Twayne's United States Authors Series

Sylvia E. Bowman, *Editor*

INDIANA UNIVERSITY

Stephen Crane

STEPHEN CRANE.

by EDWIN H. CADY
Indiana University

TWAYNE PUBLISHERS
A DIVISION OF G. K. HALL & CO., BOSTON Mass.

FOR FRAN

Contents

Preface

A S HAS BEEN repeatedly remarked by long-lived critics, Stephen Crane has been repeatedly "rediscovered." The situation calls for a new definition of neglect, said John Winterich ten years ago.[1] That cycle may, however, be permanently broken by Crane's current recognition as a major, standard American author. He has become the object of a small literary industry, a "field," as a glance at the bibliography at the rear of this volume will show. He is here to stay.

And yet, as has also been said before, Crane appeared to pass through the culture of his time like a visitant from outer space. The facts about him are as brief and in some essentials obscure, the explanation of his brilliance is as conjectural, as the annals of a comet. He was the first "modern" writer to come on the American scene. Yet it is surprising to realize how much we do not know about him. The dates, and therefore the sequence of some of his most crucial acts and writings, are obscure. We know almost nothing about his reading. The qualities and meaning of many of his personal contacts are clouded. Key anecdotes about the man come from undocumentable hearsay or long-delayed reminiscence. Many are contradictory or otherwise dubious. Therefore much of what is "understood" about Stephen Crane is highly—if not wildly— conjectural, unreliable, and possibly absurd. He has made a handy peg upon which to hang pet theories or myths.

Since we cannot help ourselves, no one need be too distressed by our necessity of guessing at the truth about Crane. At best, the facts would, aside from what intrinsic value his biography contains, help us to read his literature more profoundly, more rewardingly, perhaps more exactly. But no one works long with biography or with literary analysis before deserting any "scientific" notions he might have had about the attainment of Truth and taking up instead some ideal closer to the juridical ideal of justice: to get a pattern of impressions which is just, fair, and in the closest possible harmony with the whole picture of the subject's career and art.

Frankly admitting the probable deficiencies of my own perceptions, I undertook to write this book because it seemed to me that certain aspects of the most generally accepted picture of Crane were less than just, even given the difficulties of knowledge already referred to. It was my aim to attempt to present Crane in his present situation and posture, as he may be seen. Quarreling as little as possible with others and not attempting to clinch the case for my view, I hope to stimulate, possibly by unsettling received ideas, fresh judgments.

Amid all the controversy and contradiction over Stephen Crane, somebody must be wrong. But of the work of the major students of Crane I should say that, barring minor points, I have thought it not mistaken, not wrongheaded or blundering—on the contrary!—but partial, inclined to oversimplification for the sake of harmony of view. Crane, in short, appears more complex, less categorizable than presented. He has been psychographically oversimplified, and by lay analysts. He has been neglected as athlete, sportsman, and outdoorsman; as an intellectual of his age; as aspiring gentleman and moralist; and even (odd though this may sound in his case) as an existentialist saint for all time. He has been mutilated on the iron frame of many a Procrustean "-ist" when, as I see him, he remained an uncrystallized experimenter, a youthful pluralist. And interpretations of his work have been tyrannized by unitary views of the man and mind.

With those aims in view, chapters one and two survey Crane's life, aiming to bring out considerations the biographical tradition has hitherto neglected or misemphasized. Chapter three studies Crane's ideas as I think no one has previously done. And the final three chapters undertake to summarize the principal modes of Crane criticism and to match their trends of judgment against my own considered responses to Crane's literary art.

If I succeed at all in promoting more balance and complication, more pluralistic richness, and more versatility in view of Crane and his art, I shall have succeeded indeed. And, as is usually true, I shall have owed that success in large part to others. Apart from the Crane scholars and critics acknowledged in the "Notes" and annotated in the bibliography, I am particularly grateful to the following persons: Norma W. Cady, who worked, coped, and above all understood, as she always does;

the young lady to whom this book is dedicated, whose friendship I value more than ever with the years; Richard Baldwin, E. Fred Carlisle, and Michael Fowler, for research help; James M. Cox, Albert J. George, Terence Martin, Jack Lunn Mowers, Lester G. Wells, and William E. Wilson, for reading this manuscript; Lester G. Wells and the Stephen Crane Collection, Lena R. Arents Rare Book Room, Syracuse University Library; the staffs and collections of the Clifton Waller Barrett Collection, Alderman Library, University of Virginia; the Lilly and University Libraries, Indiana University; the Houghton Library, Harvard; and the Columbia University Library.

A grant for research travel and assistance from the Graduate Research Division of the Indiana University Graduate School, John W. Ashton, Dean and Vice-President, is gratefully acknowledged.

EDWIN H. CADY

Rudy Professor of English
Indiana University

Acknowledgments

FOR PERMISSION to quote copyrighted or otherwise privileged materials, thanks are hereby extended to the following: Alfred A. Knopf, Inc., holder of the literary rights to Stephen Crane's letters, manuscripts, etc., for general permission to quote from such materials and, more specifically, for permission to quote from Thomas Beer, *Stephen Crane*, 1923; and Robert W. Stallman, ed., *Stephen Crane: An Omnibus*, 1952. The Syracuse University Press, for permission to quote from Edwin H. Cady and Lester G. Wells, eds., *Stephen Crane's Love Letters to Nellie Crouse*, 1954; Melvin Schoberlin, ed., *The Sullivan County Sketches of Stephen Crane*, 1949; Corwin K. Linson, *My Stephen Crane*, 1958. The New York University Press for permission to quote from Robert W. Stallman and Lillian Gilkes, *Stephen Crane: Letters*, 1960.

Also to the Clifton Waller Barrett Collection of the Alderman Library, the University of Virginia for permission to examine and quote from the manuscript of *The Red Badge of Courage* and Stephen Crane's pocket notebook; and to the Lilly Library, Indiana University for permission to quote the corrected inscription on the cover of Hamlin Garland's copy of the first edition of *Maggie*; to *ELH* and the Johns Hopkins Press for permission to reprint from my article "Stephen Crane and 'the Strenuous Life'"; and to the Trustees of the Remington Art Memorial, Ogdensburg, New York, for the letter of Frederic Remington to William Dean Howells.

Chronology

1871   Stephen Crane born November 1, in Newark, New Jersey, fourteenth and last child of the Rev. Dr. Jonathan Townley Crane and Mary Helen Peck Crane.

1878   Dr. Crane assumes Methodist pastorate in Port Jervis, New York; Stephen begins his first schooling in the town which would become his "Whilomville."

1880   Jonathan Townley Crane dies, February 16.

1883   Mrs. Crane moves with Stephen to Asbury Park, New Jersey.

1888   Stephen enrolls as student at Hudson River Institute [and Claverack College], Claverack, New York. In summer begins to assist brother Townley Crane with his Press Bureau at Asbury Park.

1890   Stephen enters Lafayette College as engineering student, September 12; joins Delta Upsilon fraternity; fails course and leaves after Christmas vacation.

1891   Registers, January 9, at Syracuse University; plays catcher and shortstop on varsity baseball team; reports for newspapers; attends few classes; probably drafts earliest state of *Maggie*. In summer meets Hamlin Garland after reporting Garland lecture on realism. Does not return to college in fall but tries to establish self in New York City. Mary Helen Peck Crane dies, December 7.

1892   Fails to hold newspaper jobs. Serial publication of seven "Sullivan County Sketches."

1893   Private printing, paid for by Crane, of *Maggie: A Girl of the Streets*; through Garland, gains friendship of William Dean Howells. Begins *The Red Badge of Courage*.

1894   Begins writing poems. Begins *George's Mother*. "An Experiment in Misery" and "An Experiment in Luxury" published. *The Red Badge* published (abridged) by Bacheller Syndicate in newspapers.

1895   Crane starts West to report for Bacheller. Final revision of *The Red Badge* made in New Orleans; to Mexico, March 12. *The Black Riders* published May 11. *The Red Badge of Courage* published October 5; by December, Crane an international literary celebrity.

1896   *George's Mother*; *Maggie*; *The Little Regiment*; *The Third Violet*, various other stories and some poems all published. Crane becomes butt of envious, malicious gossip in New York: the Dora Clark case makes him victim of persecution by police; to Jacksonville, Florida, as correspondent to Cuban insurrection, November; meets Cora Taylor.

1897   January 2, shipwrecked from *Commodore* off Florida coast; "The Open Boat" published June. To Greece (accompanied by Cora Taylor) to report Turkish war (April-May). To England, with Cora as "Mrs. Crane"; writes "The Monster," "The Bride Comes to Yellow Sky," "Death and the Child," and "The Blue Hotel" between June and the following February. Meets Joseph Conrad.

1898   *The Open Boat and Other Tales of Adventure.* To the United States to volunteer for Spanish-American war service; rejected by Navy, goes as war correspondent for Pulitzer; involves self as daringly as possible in combat action at Guantanamo, Cuzco, Las Guasimas, San Juan Hill; writes some of war's best dispatches; invalided home and discharged, returns at once for Hearst to Puerto Rico; "disappears" into Havana to write, perhaps recuperate. To New York in November.

1899   To England where Cora had manorial "Brede Place" and a mountain of their debts waiting for him; writes desperately to catch up. *War Is Kind*; *Active Service*; *The Monster and Other Stories* published. At big Christmas Week houseparty Crane suffers massive tubercular hemorrhage.

1900   *Whilomville Stories*; *Wounds in the Rain*; *Great Battles of the World* published. Crane works on *The O'Ruddy* (finished by Robert Barr, 1903) and the pieces which appeared as *Last Words*, 1902. Dies, Badenweiler, Germany, June 5.

Stephen Crane

The Ghost of Chatterton

THOMAS CHATTERTON, the "marvellous boy" of Bristol, drank arsenic in a London garret in 1770 to still his starving stomach and bitter heart. By that act the gifted hoaxer turned himself into a potent ghost. He became the type-hero of a number of myths essential to the romantic views of genius: of the poet crushed by his culture; of the personality in death-wish peril from the creative impulse; of the warfare between a religious, holistic past and an esthetic, fragmented modernity—of, in short, the tragic fate of the artist. Successively Chatterton's ghost claimed German romantic poets and composers; Shelley's "Adonaïs" and then Shelley, Byron, and eventually Poe; then in lengthening files Rimbaud, Hart Crane, Garcia Lorca and others.

That is a very romantic regiment. And Stephen Crane, who mainly hated romanticism, would doubtless have been moved to complex ironies at being placed in it. Yet, ironically, his principal biographers, Thomas Beer, John Berryman, and Louis Zara, are quite right in portraying Crane as Chattertonian. He "sprang into life fully armed," as Howells wonderingly affirmed. He blazed intensely, even scandalously, on the public scene. He burned up perhaps his genius and certainly his life-force early. He was dead before he became twenty-nine. No matter how much he might, in the forefront of his mind, have scorned the idea, Crane's life stands historically (as perhaps deep in his mind it did really) subject to the ghost of Chatterton.[1]

I

Stephen, born on the first of November, 1871, was the ninth survivor among the fourteen children of the Reverend Doctor Jonathan Townley Crane and Mary Helen Peck Crane. He was thus the late, last darling of a big family, the babe of his parents' age; and he was both blest and doomed to the life of what the denominational colleges branded "a PK"—a Preacher's Kid. Dr. Crane, as presiding elder (what would now be called District Superintendent) of the Newark, New Jersey, district of the Methodist Episcopal Church, was a beloved and weighty servant. He had labored for his Lord as preacher, teacher, school and area administrator, writer, and pastor. Success had corrupted neither his sacrificial spirit, his admired sense of humor, nor the gentleness of his thought and feelings. His brilliant boy, no doubt mistakenly, would later suppose him to have been simply innocent of evil. As Christian, scholar, and gentleman, Jonathan Crane is more likely merely to have thought evil overrated.

Stephen's mother naturally made an excellent parsonage wife. She was the daughter and sister of a redoubtable tribe of upstate New York Methodist preachers. The Pecks had moved from the years of back-woods exhorting to those of booming industrialism without much altering their camp-meeting tough mindedness or their minatory language.

Dr. Crane, however, had become a Methodist in rebellion against the fierceness of his Presbyterian heritage and in defiance of a Princeton education. It was in the spirit of Horace Bushnell, not of Peter Cartwright, that he wrote his books. To promote love, redemption, and Christian nurture, he had warned against the dangers of *Popular Amusements* (1869) and *Arts of Intoxication* (1870). But the core of his thought he expressed in *Holiness the Birthright of all God's Children* (1874). It was, as Daniel Hoffman has shown, rather against the essentially vulgar damnation-evangel of the Pecks than against his father's thought that Stephen would revolt.

The essence of Stephen Crane's situation was that he must revolt. The laconic penetration of collegiate wit produced the brand "PK" as a sufficient explanation for eccentric, defiant behavior. Was some classmate, often attractive and gifted, running wild? Oh, just another "PK." After eighteen years of genteel poverty, of tyranny from the Official Board, the Ladies' Aid, and the Eye of the Community, of parental meekness toward the tyrants and suppression if not oppression of the child; after ten or a dozen moves, each into somebody else's house in a new town with an unknown and therefore less predictable set of tyrants; after a lifetime of newness in eight or nine different schools, with the problems of the new children in his peer group intolerably intensified by his being the mysterious, sacrosanct, and therefore easily hated minister's child; after years of loneliness and repression, it was not to be wondered that at college the liberated not infrequently broke into strange patterns of revolt in the effort to define and discover themselves. Even in narrow, unsophisticated denominational colleges people developed a special wisdom and tolerance in forbearing with "PK's."

And theirs was, on the whole, the early fate of Stephen Crane. His father changed districts in 1872 and moved his family in 1874. He left administration for a pastorate in Paterson, New Jersey, and moved his home in 1876. He left the metropolitan area in 1878 to move to a final church in leafy Port Jervis at the hilly meeting point of New York, New Jersey, and Pennsylvania. That final move may have been out of care for the frail health of blond, spindly Stevie. And Stevie went to school for the first time in Port Jervis that September, almost seven years old, securely literate, and so furiously humiliated at being put with the first-graders that he jumped two grades in six weeks. With his peers in Port Jervis he experienced those militant intricacies of boyhood in a deceptively simple small town which were amply documented by Thomas Bailey Aldrich, Mark Twain, and William Dean Howells before they were reimaged by Stephen Crane, author of *The Whilomville Stories* (1900). But in Crane the after-nostalgia for "Whilom" was sharpened by the fact that his "happy childhood" in Port Jervis was intolerably brief. After some eighteen months of Dr. Crane's usual success in the new church, that tired saint suddenly died on February 16, 1880, and Stephen Crane became an orphan at eight.

II

Much of the amateur-Freudian speculation that this or that literary invention of Crane represents revolt against his father must face the simple fact that Stephen never knew his father well. With what images of father he grew up, we shall never know exactly. But there are items in Crane's heritage from that good man which can be reasonably evidenced. What Stephen was to make of his heritage is not yet to the point. Its very content may be seen as, predictably, religious and moral concern, a care for personal cultivation and expression, and, perhaps less expectedly, certain ideals of aristocracy. All of these conspired to intensify the isolation from common experience already sprung from the social situation of the preacher's kid.

That none of the other eight surviving Crane children became particularly distinguished is a little surprising. Protestant ministers have contributed gifted children to the world out of all genetic ratio to their numbers. Perhaps Stephen's was a case of the superiority of a child of his parents' age. Melvin Schoberlin tells us that Stephen's nearest sibling, Agnes, was a school teacher who early promoted his reading and herself yearned to be an author. Little came of that, as of other family ambitions.

Yet nothing seems to deny that the family circle was warm nor that Jonathan and Mary Helen Crane's piety illuminated their home. Hoffman persuades one that his father's religion of love, of the inner voice and light, remained the positive base of Stephen's profoundest and nakedest metaphysical statements, those made in his poetry. Of course the father's death shocked young Stevie and left him resentful (why should anyone have been startled to find that out?). Afterward he passed through a youthful period of innocent piety; then adolescent revolt set in and he simply stopped discussing theology with a mother who argued like "a wave" for Peck ideas less humane and intelligent than Dr. Crane's. At the end of the ends, however, the point is that Stephen's religious heritage set certain focal requirements upon his vision. He couldn't *not* employ the engaged moral concern, the expectation of love, the demand for sacrifice, and the exaltation of real innocence (which Jonathan Townley Crane's religion enforced) as check points against what he thought he saw occurring in the worlds within and without.

The family care for cultivation and expression did not in itself make Stephen Crane a great writer. But it seems safe to say that he might not have turned author at all unless he had grown up among books and with people who habitually expressed themselves well. There is Beer's oft-repeated story of the towhead looking up seriously from his papers on the floor to ask, "Ma, how do you spell 'O'?" Upon application, one much-gifted graduate "PK" explained the plethora of talent in the type by saying, in effect: "We never had a house of our own. We never had good things to sleep on or eat off. People gave us all sorts of ugly things, and we had to take them. But we did have books. All the good young people came to our house to talk. We cared for ideas and such art as we knew and cared terribly."

Certainly the known facts about the Crane family concern for cultivation go far toward explaining the mystery of Stephen's artistic mastery in the face of his weak formal education. Clearly he had learned the essential thing—how to use books to his purpose—without, if not in spite of, his colleges. It is arguable that he was better off with his quality of self-education than any academic program could have made him. At least that was what his contemporary Robert Frost discovered in his own case.

"The new baby is a boy and we have named him Stephen for his ancestor who signed the Declaration," wrote Dr. Crane the morning after his last son's birth. If the ancestor did not actually sign the Declaration of Independence, he might have. Himself descended from an original Stephen who had settled Elisabethtown, New Jersey, in 1665 and founded a family of local gentry, that ancestor served his nascent state and republic with distinction and lost two sons (including another Stephen) in the Revolution. The writer—famous, young and with a reputation for irreverence to keep—would tell the *Newark Sunday Call* that the Cranes had been "pretty hot people" and made him "about as much of a Jerseyman as you can find." Even as he wrote that in 1896, he must have been aware that industrial megalopolis and trailing suburbia were making Old Jersey one with Tyre. Obviously, what had been a small gentry, a local aristocracy, ceased to matter when their towns and country disappeared.

Yet the sense of something fine was concealed under the flippancy of "pretty hot people." Dr. Crane had been conspicuous for gentlemanliness among his professional colleagues. Sister Agnes is known to have aspired to be a Christian lady. And it is demonstrably clear, as we shall see in Chapter three, that Stephen would to the end of his days cherish his own version of the great American ideal of the Christian gentleman.

III

If that concept would be part of the story of Stephen Crane's inner weather, there was to be a long history of outer happening before he grew up. After her husband's death, Mrs. Crane fluttered to a boardinghouse near Paterson where Stevie promptly suffered scarlet fever. Then she took him back to Port Jervis where a second cycle of Whilomville days lasted until May, 1883. Then at the age of eleven, he was taken to complete his boyhood education in the fatefully appropriate town of Asbury Park, New Jersey.

Naming it for Francis Asbury, the great circuit-riding true founder of their church in America, the Methodists had established Asbury Park, a resort on the beaches of southern New Jersey. Connecting directly to the south was the rigidly controlled conference center of Ocean Grove, and just below that the Chautauqua-type cultural center of Avon-by-the-Sea. Thither Mrs. Crane was drawn, apparently by the prospect of summer employment as a speaker to Methodist women's groups. Her son Townley had a reasonably successful news agency, and the family was reorganized about as well as might have been hoped after the father's death. At Asbury Park, Stephen was at least somewhat free of the burdens of the preacher's kid, and the location held wonderful potentialities for education in the world of the American *fin de siècle*.

Its setting, of course, presented—the thundering surf on the white sand beach, the ships and ocean weather—materials to absorb which would some day make Crane one of the great writers of the sea. But the human phenomena the setting attracted around him also taught Stephen severe lessons in double standards of morality. To that rural isolation of sea, sand, and empty back country were drawn crowds of visitors parading wealth, vulgarity or sophistication, and self-indulgent leisure. Naturally there was the tension normal in resort towns between natives and tourists, exploiters and exploited, hustlers and suckers. To have any glimpse from the inside of the processes thus involved makes for cynicism; and Crane was by temperament, by childhood training as a preacher's kid, and by the nature of his own slightly detached situation in the town, supremely an observer. But the discrepancies of appearance and reality in Asbury Park were redoubled by its official, ecclesiastical status. It was hard to keep Asbury Park from becoming just a fun town accentuating the difference between saints and sinners, Methodists and worldlings. Its resident founder and czar had to fight against too much freedom from wintertime conventions. Sex, both as prostitution and as vacation assignations, liquor, and gambling kept edging in. Young people found a sordid sanctuary under the boardwalk.

Riding his pony over the beaches and back through the brush and eventually pursuing news items for Townley, Stephen Crane came to know the area intimately. Thomas Beer records the story that Stephen once saw a white girl stabbed by her Negro lover. He stayed away from prayer meetings (except when he gladdened his mother's heart by unexpectedly attending after being made tipsy by his first introduction to the red *vino* of a "nefarious Florentine"). He took up with the local sporting crowd, swiftly developing a passion for baseball (flouting his father's cautions against popular amusements). Sometime in this period his mother almost completely lost control over him. When he left Asbury Park for military school at the age of fifteen or sixteen, he was a confirmed smoker. Not only had Dr. Crane upon *Arts of Intoxication* been set at nought; Stephen was flying in the face of all Methodism, to say nothing of official Asbury Park.

IV

Perhaps it is significant that Crane in after years went back to Port Jervis for "Whilom" friends far more readily than to Asbury Park. It was his fate never to have a hometown or even, in the sense of place, a home. Strong inner activity, especially reverie life and reading, must have compensated. The Asbury Park years—roughly his twelfth to seventeenth—would have been decisive in any life; in Crane's they were evidently fateful. They confirmed in the sensitive, vulnerable, fatherless preacher's kid his fate as *isolato*. He learned to make outward, comradely terms with the world of men, but not with that of women, as an overtly masculine figure. He played games, especially baseball, with fiendish drive; he smoked and swore ostentatiously; he gloried in the appearance of what was evil to his elders. But careful observers noted that he lit cigarettes and let them burn to ashes in his stained fingers, that he slid a drink around on a bar and left it unconsumed.

Stephen Crane in the Asbury Park years became elaborately conformed to his present world in some of its obviously "un-Christian" ways. But actually he was *in* but not *of* it. Inwardly and truly he was an *isolato,* a stranger and a sojourner, a spy in the world. He was not, of course, therefore a Christian. He was admirably preparing to become an artist. *Isolato*-rebel, rebel-*isolato*—who could say which quite came first, though each condition bred the other? The immediate fact was that his mother had lost control of him, and she no doubt began to have open as well as intuitive evidence of the fact.

The time-honored solution was to send the boy away to school. Apparently Mrs. Crane first tried the Pennington Seminary of which Dr. Crane had been principal for ten years before the Civil War, and that parental surrogate failed promptly. Next, according to L. U. Pratt, on January 4, 1888, Stephen arrived at the Hudson River Institute in Claverack, New York, with a rack of big pipes and a surface so tough he immediately moved into the leadership circle. It occurred to nobody to think him a parsonage sissy.

Actually, the three and a half years which took him from entrance to Claverack at sixteen to exit from Syracuse in June, 1891, at nineteen, were all of a piece. They formed an essential middle of the education which began on the boardwalk at Asbury Park and finished among the Bowery bums and Bohemians of Old New York in about 1894, when he was twenty-two or twenty-three.

The institution Crane liked to call "old C.C." (because it had absorbed the moribund Claverack College) was a somewhat indeterminate institution—a military prep school with vestiges of a junior college. It gave Crane four very important things: military experience, academic training, the collegiate feeling, and athletic achievement. Ironically (as his entire preparation for life was to be ironic), it cheated him on all of its first three gifts. And no doubt he knew it. Its military character was make-believe. Its academic training was amateurish even by the feeble standards of the day. In an age when college life first became a glamorous public reality in the United States, Claverack could offer only an impoverished, distantly improvised imitation. Only the athletics were "real." College seemed as phony as Asbury Park.

What was confirmed therefore by his college was the baffling figure of Crane the floating, *déclassé* aristocrat. "Stevie is like the wind in Scripture," sighed Mrs. Crane. "He bloweth whither he listeth." "After all, I cannot help vanishing and disappearing and dissolving," wrote Crane at the height of success. "It is my foremost trait."[2]

As a type, the self-conscious *déclassé* is a figure far more important to the genesis of American literature than has ever been realized. To name only some obvious ones, his characteristics have been shared by Freneau, Cooper, Poe, Emerson, Hawthorne, Melville, Henry James, and Scott Fitzgerald. Orphaned, impoverished, disinherited, clear superiority denied or disregarded, he often knew drear November in his soul. Communication with the world being impossible, he withdrew to mighty dreams and to scornful observation of the herd. Alienation taught him that elusive, floating quality. And it inclined him to moods ambiguously self-pitying and ironic. In the keenest minds the irony became double-edged; it turned back upon the posturing self and bit deep.

It ought to go without saying that personal histories and temperaments made for wide individual variations of the type. But Crane was never to outlive his extraordinarily representative purity. Ford Madox Ford noticed in him "a great deal of the defiant mistrust that the French called *méfiance*," and a striking ability to play exasperating roles.[3] And we are lucky to have recorded from Claverack days the sensitive but maliciously cold-fish vision of Crane registered by a painter, Harvey Wickham.

Wickham was drilled in Company C of the student battalion by "1st Lieutenant" Crane and never forgave his officer's "perfectly hen-like attitude toward the rank and file." The implication is that Crane's ardor for drilling his company to victory in the yearly Review was not shared by Wickham and that the Private discovered that "Stevie was not tender of other people's vanities." Wickham's unhappy eye saw that, though Crane went around "in a dirty old sweater," his chum was "the richest boy in school" and dressed "in the height of collegiate fashion." Wickham the esthete baited Crane into his choir in the village Methodist church with red-haired Harriet Mathison. "He had a light, pleasant voice, true in pitch, if of no very great power or compass," Wickham judged. He saw that, though Crane talked only of "poker and baseball" in a tone suggesting *noblesse oblige*," he had to tread very softly with the authorities. He detected Crane's profound "fear of ridicule, especially of his own." And he concluded of Stevie that "all his life he strove to win recognition as a regular fellow . . . and he failed. Only women and hero worshippers ever really liked him [the exception was other artists, but warmed-over resentments barred the grown Wickham from the grown Crane]. He wanted to be a democrat and yet a dictator. Hence that contradiction, self-depreciation coupled with arrogance . . . his chum was the richest boy in school."

That damnable iteration about roommate Earl Reeves's money sufficiently betrays Wickham. His malice veiled the whole truth, but it revealed portions a kindlier eye might not have seen. The friendlier view would have noted the earnestness of the boy who went about drawling, "Ho, hell." He fell madly in love also with Jennie Pierce and made, as he later recalled, "a pure complete ass" of himself. He played baseball well enough to have to decline the captaincy of the team. He was gazetted Captain of Company C. It was "the happiest period of my life although I was not then aware of it," he wrote one of the Claverack co-eds all of six years later.[4] But even then he was *in*, not *of* it.

His *méfiance* was directed at the academic conventions of college life. Bawling stage-drivers and baggage-smashers in Arkansas, he wrote in 1895, were "as unintelligible as a row of Homeric experts."[5] But his portraits in *Active Service* of student high-jinks are as contemptuous as are those of the heroine's professor-father. And when he went, presumably in response to maternal practicality, to study mining-engineering at Lafayette instead of returning to Claverack in 1890, he defined himself unforgettably in reaction against the conventions of student life.

Lafayette was very much "Old Siwash" in its attitudes. Crane started in acceptably enough by joining the Delta Upsilon fraternity. But the next week a band of hazing sophomores came to "get" him at his dormitory room. When he refused to open it, they broke down the door—and stopped. A later-arriving witness saw that "Steve was petrified with fear and stood in a grotesque nightgown in one corner of the room with a revolver in his hand. His usual sallow complexion seemed to be a ghastly green . . . both arms were limp and the revolver was pointed to the floor."[6] That might have been panic from the start. It might more likely have been Crane's shock proceeding from the realization that he had nearly murdered somebody. Crane was hazed no more.

By Christmas, Stephen had effectively flunked out of Lafayette; and a family council during the vacation apparently determined to enter him at Syracuse, which had been founded largely by his mother's uncle, the late Bishop Jesse Peck.

As soon as he could get out of the Widow Peck's house and into the Delta Upsilon lodge, Crane began to find Syracuse more *simpático* in all ways not academic—"although the fellows here *are* somewhat slow," he confided back to "old C. C."[7] It was a "dandy house" in a "dandy city," and there were "some damn pretty girls" around. There were also enough Claverackians to make up an alumni association, of which Crane became secretary-treasurer, and some old chums from Port Jervis. Some of the slow Methodists forced him and other smokers into the chilly cupola so as not to have the house tainted by the fumes. But they accepted the deliberately scandalous Stevie, according him the notorious liberties of the "P. K."

The faculty tried letting him have his head as a special student; gave him an "A" in the only course he completed (English literature under Chancellor Charles N. Sims); let his first published tale appear in *The University Herald*; and made him permanently, if not immediately, grateful by trying tactfully to snatch his brand from the burning. The students let him star on a winning varsity baseball team; let him bully them a bit socially and bully-rag them a bit about police courts, journalism, and real life; and apparently enjoyed his iconoclasm. His nicotine-stained fingers and tough poses and his telling professors that he knew what St. Paul said but disagreed with him and, more cogently, that Miss Frances Willard, the sentimental reformer, was "a fool," no doubt set up mild shock-waves. But the Methodists appear, after their fashion, to have understood.

The college annual, *The Onondagan*, gaily listed Stephen Crane in a column headed "Grinds" and illustrated with a little garland of memorial verse:

> Sweet drop of pure and pearly light,
> In thee the rays of virtue shine,
> More calmly clear, more mildly bright
> Than any gem that gilds the mine.

The tribute was a memorial because Crane was gone. He would spend an important summer reporting Asbury Park news for his brother Townley and the *New York Tribune*. He would take an important camping trip with Port Jervis boys. But he left Syracuse with an understanding with one of them, Fred Lawrence, that they would not return. Next fall Lawrence would begin medical study in New York and Steve would go along and room with him: not for medical study, but, as the antique statement runs, to seek his fortune—perhaps journalism, perhaps literature, perhaps. . . .

His formal education was over.

V

In the fall his real education decisively began in New York. It was to lead to a dark and complex knowledge of the life and nature of man; to an astonishing flowering in the command of an art (his datable writing thus far had been sophomoric); to stark privation of body and psyche through long and bitter discipline, agony, and defeat to breathtaking victory. And to the knowledge, final with Crane, that the priceless victory was prizeless and empty.

He began life in New York as he mostly continued in failure or success, stony broke. Perhaps nothing is so basic to an understanding of Stephen Crane's life as a clear grasp of how he handled money and of what that means. But to date there have come to light virtually no records. The impression one gets is that he lived by a wholly Bohemian code—borrowing and cadging when he had no money, wholly open-handed to others when he had. But there seems to be no way of proving that or anything else about the subject.

The dates and sequences of many events in these crucial years are obscure. Apparently Stephen began to ease into New York by living with his brother Edmund in Lake View, New Jersey, within easy commuting distance. From there he could make forays to the city for job-hunting, for getting up studies for free-lance articles, for seeing people, and for studying the new life of man in polyglot, industrial megalopolis. It was apparently all right at "Ed's house" if he disappeared for days at a time while staying with some friend who had a "place" in the city. William Dean Howells, who did not yet know Crane, would begin in March, 1892, to publish chapters of a novel keenly prescient of Crane's situation: *The World of Chance.*

The great curse of Victorian Christianity was its inability to distinguish between humanity and respectability. The effects, bad enough in green Port Jervis and queer Asbury Park, were catastrophic in the cities. There the poor and outcast swarmed in their immigrant and proletarian millions. Like the cities, these people were phenomena of the industrialization of Western life which had overwhelmed the older culture with massive problems for which it had few and feeble solutions. Precisely because the churches had largely chosen to ignore these throngs and their problems, Stephen Crane, one guesses, chose to join those who were determined to confront, explore, and understand.

While Crane was at Claverack, Howells had set the country tingling with *A Hazard of New Fortunes,* a novel which insisted that we not "forget" the poor, the agonized, the trapped in screaming megalopolis. It scarified with its ironies both those who would not remember and those who could not bring themselfes to be compassionate with the poor as persons. It dramatized with power the situation of the rising number of those who were seeking to go down to the slums and help. Whatever his immediate impulses, Crane seems to have begun to go down himself from Piety Hill to the canal waterfront slums in Syracuse and to write of what he saw in streets, saloons, and police court.

But the ideal place was New York. Everything was bigger, intenser, and worse there. And worst of all was the Bowery. It was, Crane protested to Miss Helen Trent, an older beauty with whom he fell disastrously in love late in the summer of 1891, "the most interesting place in New York." And he was studying it so intimately he showed up one night with a shiner acquired when a stray beer bottle thrown in a saloon fight hit him in the eye. He was mastering the technique for studying people and places. He took advantage of protective coloration: "the youthful stranger with the blonde and innocent hair,"[8] as he once described himself. He was inconspicuous, silent but a good listener who encouraged talk, an expert stalker of his game. A wartime correspondent was fascinated afterwards to watch Crane's perfect technique. He could associate with thieves and cutthroats, even in foreign ports, and never be harmed. He sat "soaking in knowledge of the reactions of the kind of men he liked to write about . . . a sombre, silent member, contributing no adventure of his own, never flushing his quarry with a word that was not in their vocabulary."[9] He bagged his game.

Such *expertise* came slowly, of course. And its mastery, as well as its exercise in "human interest" vignettes of increasing literary but low news value, interfered with Crane's thrust toward professional journalism. He had worked as a "stringer" on various papers since going to Claverack. A quite possible solution to the problem of a career—even one which might at length support literature—was newspaper work. In 1891 he was a really valuable part of his brother Townley's news agency from Asbury Park, and he found a job as stringer on the *New York Tribune*. In August, caught in an absurd episode with Asbury correspondence for the *Tribune*, he got himself fired and Townley's agency ruined. Briefly in early 1892 he held but lost a job with the *Herald*. It became clear that he was to have no salaried "basis" for other writing in journalism.

The reasons for his lack of acceptance as a journalist are complex and a little obscure. Mere reporting—"Who-What-Where-When-How Much"—bored Crane. To "Why-How-How-it-Felt," he responded passionately. But that was for stars, not cubs. The rude disciplines of the near-chaotic offices disgusted him. His study and respond method, slowly mastered, eventually made him a superb feature writer. When studying a fire, a traffic jam, an epileptic down in the street, a drunk, a restaurant, Coney Island, the crowds and what they said and did, and the police who vaguely ruled them, Crane commanded his New York as few artists have ever done and as no one else before the Ashcan painters did. In an informal will which he wrote on the way to his "Open Boat" adventure in 1896, he said accurately to his brother William, "Some of my best work is contained in short things which I have written for various publications. . . . There are some fifteen or twenty short sketches of New York street life and so on which I intended to have published in book form under the title of 'Midnight Sketches.' That should be your first care." Midnight sketches were fine training for literature but not for reporting.

Another contributing factor to his lack of success as a journalist may have been that Crane simply didn't get along with reporters. Samuel Hopkins Adams grew sharp when remembering how cordially "the boys" in New York in the '90's detested Crane. His friends were the circle of old Claverack and Port Jervis chums and other artists—writers, painters, actors. To reporters he seemed aloof, "stuck up," arty, snooty, and spoiled. When opportunity offered, they would lay for him in the "paragraphs." One suspects that to him they seemed frantic and corrupt—and that they caught him studying them. At any rate, he was forced into a life of preparation for becoming an artist. He had all the time there was to learn to see with his own eyes and find the words to create the same vision in the mind of a reader. And he could rewrite, revise, and write again the story he had crudely begun at Syracuse about a girl of the streets.

From a strictly artistic point of view, this almost pure apprenticeship might seem all to the good. Other things being equal, it was almost ideal. But there was one key factor wholly out of balance: money. With deliberate stoicism, Crane suffered bitter physical privation, through the winters, particularly, of 1892-1893 and 1893-1894. He was in no danger of "forgetting" the sufferings of the poor in the slums. He shared them to learn and practice his art and, in the pathetic, infuriating case of the 1893 *Maggie,* to publish it. He lived in virtual madhouse dormitories of medical students and then of artists. He sponged on strugglers only a little less impecunious for a bed, for a meal, for a little warmth, quiet, and relative privacy in which to write. He wore his shoes to tatters for want of carfare and days came when he couldn't go out because he could no longer patch the holes with paper—he was literally "on his uppers." Parts of *The Red Badge of Courage* he wrote "on the paper the meat came home in."[10] He went ill-clad and cold. Penniless, he actually starved at times, and he was malnourished for much of three years.

Some of his deprivation resulted from pride. When he came to the point of collapse, there was always a Linson, a Vosburgh, a Gordon, a Garland to bail him out. He was welcome at his brothers' houses and repeatedly retreated to Ed's at Lake View and later Hartwood, New York, or to Will's at Port Jervis. But how often can a self-respecting man be bailed out? How often, how much can he borrow? How long can he practice his art and admit it will not feed him? No doubt some of Crane's agony also proceeded from improvidence. And yet—was it really improvidence to risk all on printing *Maggie?* What's provident? Can the life of an artist truly be so in an acquisitive culture? Financially-shrewd Howells thought not. Modern nations are finding ways to subvent their artists and starve no more Chattertons, Schuberts, Cranes.

Whether pride or art or character caused it, Crane's suffering was real; and it produced important effects. It ruined his teeth, wracked his body, and doubtless presented him the tuberculosis which eventually killed him. It also affected his psyche and imagination profoundly. If nothing else, it confirmed emphatically his intellectual and perhaps temperamentally necessary conviction that the condition of human life is war at every level.

VI

Bitterly losing many skirmishes and some battles, Crane sorely but steadily won through to lambent victory in his combined struggles to become a recognized artist and to deserve it. Given the circumstances, it is surprising that he persevered, wonderful that he won out, astonishing that he succeeded so early, and simply unaccountable that his level of achievement was so high. There is no better definition of genius. One famous abstract way of defining genius is the "capacity for taking infinite pains" or "application of the seat of the pants to the seat of the chair" way of describing the thrust of powerful energies. Crane had capacity to endure, but his ability to lift his art from the nonentity of his writing at Syracuse through the mixed qualities of the *Sullivan County Sketches* and "Midnight Sketches" to the achieved but various styles of *Maggie, The Black Riders,* and *The Red Badge of Courage* classically concretizes the definition of application.

But a better definition of genius is that it does prodigiously what others can do only feebly or not at all. Crane produced all this brillance between his twentieth and twenty-fifth years. This accomplishment made him another "marvelous boy," an incredible prentice. Howells found himself remembering the birth of Minerva in remarking that Crane had sprung into life fully armed.

Strictly speaking, however, Howells knew better than that. He knew what a price Crane had paid. His contact through Garland with Crane was one of the fateful inspirations of Crane's life. It began distantly when Crane heard Garland lecture at Avon-by-the-Sea in 1891 about his friend and master, Howells. Crane reported it so well for the *Tribune* that Garland looked him up. They became good enough friends for Crane to be emboldened to present Garland with a copy of the privately printed *Maggie* when Garland returned to New York. Garland, who knew Howells would like it, made Crane send him a copy. When he read it, Howells, who made a life-habit of sponsoring the young, not only liked it immensely but had Crane to tea and listened to him all evening. He began to scheme to get *Maggie* regularly published and also to read Crane's manuscripts, to see that editor's doors opened for him, to publicize him as judiciously as he could.

Howells was the reigning Dean of American letters. His critical arm was the longest and strongest in the nation. No one he sponsored as a brilliant young man remained unknown. His endorsement was that most courted and angled after. To Crane it came through merit (and the agony of printing *Maggie*) and with it was Howells' warm friendship. Crane testified repeatedly to the warmth of his response. Garland and Howells seem to have nerved, even in part inspired, him to the achievement of the 1893-95 period which made him great.

Even with Howells' help, Crane continued to be jinxed for a crucial while. Not all the Dean's personal intervention would persuade booksellers to push *Maggie*; and even B. O. Flower, the reform editor, somehow failed to republish it, though Garland reviewed it in Flower's *Arena*. Crane sold nothing at all in 1893. But he had the courage and encouragement to go on. He wrote short stories about the doomed baby, Tommie, from *Maggie*. He and a painter friend, Corwin Knapp Linson, tried collaborating on an illustrated version of Crane's humor, "The Reluctant Voyagers," and Linson was thrilled to pick Steve up one morning and find him wearily concluding an all-night sitting which produced "The Pace of Youth." Still nothing would sell.

In desperation Crane thought of turning out a pot-boiler—a historical romance about the Civil War. He began to do research in, among other places, Linson's studio, where copies of the *Century Magazine's* "Battles and Leaders of the Civil War" lay handy to the divan and there was shelter out of the cold, spring rains and quiet while Linson worked. But it was clear almost from the beginning that Crane was incapable of the more lucrative swashbucklering. In the midst of Linson's silent sketching one day, Crane, "squatting like an Indian among the magazines," blew up: "I wonder that *some* of these fellows don't tell how they *felt* in those scraps! They spout eternally of what they *did*, but they are as emotionless as rocks!" He would need to work his imagination through the whole spectrum of "how they *felt*" before he would know why they did not talk about emotion. When he had done so, *The Red Badge of Courage* would be very popular. It would also be the work of a serious artist, not a hack.

Nobody knows how many versions Crane wrote of *The Red Badge*. One can document seven "states" of the manuscript from surviving pages, but obviously much went before. Linson says that a first draft was done in March, 1893, and "the full manuscript" completed at Lake View the following summer. Whether that second draft is the one which survives fragmentarily on the verso of its successor nobody knows. When Crane came back to town in the fall wearing rubber boots because his shoes were gone, he had a treasure in manuscript form. But he was several times on the point of collapse before fortune finally shifted.

Until it did, however, he moved, as a kind of ward of a bunch of "Indians" of young artists, into the old Art Students' League Building. There, perhaps because hearing Howells read the poetry of the newly discovered Emily Dickinson had unlocked fresh creative impulses,[11] Crane began suddenly to write poetry in defiance of the yowling jeers of the "Indians." Of course it was not poetry like Dickinson's; her revolution had only unleashed his. And his was still more *outré*:

> In the desert
> I saw a creature, naked, bestial,
> Who, squatting upon the ground,
> Held his heart in his hands,
> And ate of it.
> I said, "Is it good, friend?"
> "It is bitter,—bitter," he answered;
> "But I like it
> Because it is bitter,
> And because it is my heart."

The imagery was often surrealistic as well as dramatic, and the "lining"—the special gift of knowing just where to begin and end a line—had an artistry equalled only by the greatest masters of *vers libre*.

Crane brought his poems to Linson, who was struck dumb by the procession of pictures trouping across his inner eye. He came with them to Garland, who was incredulous—and then so flabbergasted, when he discovered that Crane had a packet of the "pills" in his head and could and did sit down and write one out without pause, that he began to wonder if the right explanation were not spiritualism. Crane, however, was no "medium"; he was just a starved, almost desperate genius.¹² He was speaking out his deepest intimations about life in art as original as art ever becomes.

And still there were troubles. Not even Howells could persuade Alden of *Harpers*, an editor with whom he had worked closely for years, to buy a few poems. Nevertheless, the worst of poverty and obscurity was over. *The Arena* bought a tale and a sketch; the *New York Press* began to take Crane "specials," trumpeting their catch with a glorious interview-tribute from Howells; McClure began a promising but exasperating flirtation. John D. Barry of *Forum* volunteered to read Crane's *Lines* before the "Uncut Leaves Society" when the poet said he'd "rather die than do it" and shuddered privately while a quartet of old comrades went to see how "Lord Fauntleroy's mother" would take it. By April Crane had moved to a flat and of an evening could go with Linson and the other semi-employed for seventy-five-cent French dinners with something that passed for wine. Eating, he told Garland, was "charming." He began to negotiate with a publisher about his poems, and he had long since recovered *The Red Badge* from its "hock" to the typist (whether he ever repaid those from whom he borrowed the sum of his pawn or not).

His basic education was done. He had acquired unique literary skills, and he exercised them with a mastery acknowledged by coveted acclaim. He could hereafter expect to feed himself. If he could keep his wells of creative impulse flowing and control the personal life his bitter experience had discovered, he could hope for an absolutely major literary career. The best judges told him so.

STEPHEN CRANE

VII

There were still, of course, difficulties to come. Of his life since childhood, the summer of 1894 was perhaps the most light-hearted and appropriate for twenty-three-year old Stephen Crane. He had another slum novelette, *George's Mother*, to write and *The Red Badge* to polish. Linson and he did an article about a Scranton, Pennsylvania, coal mine for *McClure's*, which was business, fun, and enlightenment all together. In Port Jervis, Crane played for hilarious hours with Will's children and renewed his feel for "Whilomville" at an instant when his imagination was most sensitized. His sympathies for children under the tyrannies of convention were reawakened, too. When at the end of summer he was in Albany, he took a couple of little boys trapped in their mamas' adoration of Little Lord Fauntleroy's curls out and paid for their haircuts—never mind what mama would say.

And that was just after a rollicking time when, instead of the old August roughing-it group of four Port Jervis boys out in Sullivan County, New York, a couple of dozen "bob-cats" of both sexes (meticulously chaperoned) went camping in Pike County, Pennsylvania. They boated, swam, hiked, and ate standing at a long rough table "like the animals we were," Linson recalled. "In the orange light of a great campfire we gathered of evenings and perched on low branches and logs, Stephen with his back to a tree picking at a guitar." All in the out of doors they played games, flirted, and laughed—and sang, but above all, they laughed. The sportsman Crane, muscular, sanguine, identifying mystically with beautiful nature—the Crane so often forgotten and lost in the other Crane—had full play. The life was innocent, healthy, and gay.

When it was done, Crane and Louis Senger guffawed all through a night getting out a unique mock-newspaper, *The Pike County Puzzle*, to commemorate the occasion. Everybody got roasted brown, and especially "S. C." There was, for example, a note of enquiry:

What can I do with my voice? Stephen Crane.
In the spring, Stephen, you can plough with it, but after corn ripens you will have to seek employment in the blue-stone works. We have seen voices like yours used effectively for cider presses.

Perhaps that good time gave him courage to be adamant in refusing to let Copeland and Day push all the defiant religion out of the poems in *The Black Riders*. S. S. McClure kept *The Red Badge* for six months, neither finally taking it nor letting it go until Crane, justifiably, almost cracked up about it. Finally he took the manuscript away and "sold" it to Irving Bacheller's infant syndicate—sold 18,000 words of it, that is, for half a cent a word: $90. But at least it was a breakthrough, for real fame and a certain kind of fortune followed. The syndicate story ran in the *Philadelphia Press*, December 3 to 8, and in the *New York Press* all on Sunday, December 9—and, according to Berryman, in something like 750 small papers around the country. Crane heard from California about the story before Christmas, and the *Press* chain began to puff its author most flatteringly. Bacheller wanted to send him West as a roving correspondent at once, but Crane delayed—to have Christmas "at home" and to read proof on *The Black Riders*. He hung around New York through most of January, negotiating with publishers in Boston about the poems and in New York about *The Red Badge*. He got the former well settled and interested Ripley Hitchcock of Appleton's in the latter. By January 30, 1895, he was in St. Louis, poised on the threshold of the West.

A hundred years before Crane, narratives of Indian captivities designed to be uplifting accumulated prosperity for ironic reasons: they let readers by civilized firesides feel themselves part of a wilderness experience distant enough to be romantic. Then Cooper painted Hawkeye and Chingachgook. And whole cycles of the American imagination began to turn about the matter of the West. There was every reason why Stephen Crane should have known all sorts of literary Wests—in novels both serious and "dime," in the tales of strayed cowboys he had variously befriended, in *The Police Gazette*, and especially in the great magazines to which he himself aspired and in which Remington and Roosevelt and Owen Wister ruled the roost. The West was romance, wilderness, primitive simplicity, and sport—the testing of muscle, nerve, and manliness; above all, it was adventure. And wonderfully enough, Crane, the observer trained to silent nonparticipation, experienced a fascinating number of real adventures. Some were like romances, some like the Bowery, some like Remington-Roosevelt-Wister, and some could have happened only to Stephen Crane.

His first adventure was better keyed to Garland's *Main-Travelled Roads* than to Wister. From St. Louis he plunged into drought and then blizzard-blasted Dawson County, Nebraska, to report on the "Nebraskans' Bitter Fight for Life." With all the graphic power of his color and simile-laden style, he drummed up aid for the farmers brave under "the strange and unspeakable punishment of nature." He bespoke sympathy for the ill-organized Relief Commissions "involved in a mighty tangle" of "enormous difficulties" and staggering under a torment of abuse from "thugs" and self-righteous "philanthropists"—whom Crane equated. He recorded equally the plights of the abandoned horses drifting before the winds, who could not speak, and of the people eating the horses' feed who could:

> "I hain't had no aid."
> "How do you get along?"
> "Don't git along, stranger."

It made good copy for Bacheller, but it put Crane in a self-examining mood. He talked bitterly to red-haired young Willa Cather in the *Lincoln State Journal* office, and he was moved perhaps also by the fact that she was the first woman to whom he could really talk about his life and art. He had to lead a double life—reporter and artist, he said. Literature cost him infinite time and pain to filter it through his blood, to drag it out of his "hidebound" imagination. In the same mood and place he wrote Clarence Peaslee about the centrality of labor and honesty in art.

And perhaps the next night Crane learned something about the ethos of the West. Stepping between a big man and a little man punching each other in a bar fight, he was astonished to be collared by a cursing mob and dragged—for disturbing the peace—before a justice who let him off on the grounds of ignorance. It seems the two fought every night, and it was taken for granted. Crane's intended gallantry was a public nuisance. It was a story he might have invented.

En route to New Orleans he stopped over to write of the "sporting" life among "The Merry Throng at Hot Springs," Arkansas. In New Orleans he revised *The Red Badge* one last time and sent it back to Appleton's for publication. Then he headed for the land of the cowboy. There seem to have been quick touristy forays off the trains into Arizona and Nevada. Somewhere he heard the Apache scalp-dance and somewhere he acquired huge, silver spurs and "a large Smith and Wesson revolver" to match. He was well prepared for the adventure which met him on the Alamo Plaza in San Antonio in March.

There the "haunting solicitude" which a Syracuse fraternity brother remembered in Crane was wakened by sounds of sobbing from the curbstone. Edward Grover, sixteen and a runaway from Chicago with sixty dollars in birthday money to become a cowboy, was broke; rejected even by the Army, he had come to the end of his rope. Crane fed him and poured out the last of his own cash to put him on a train and to wire the boy's family. What matter that Crane would be thrown out of his hotel? It was a lot warmer than New York. His later note to Grover was perfect in its tone: "Dear Deadeye Dick: Thanks for sending back my money so fast. The hotel trun me out as my friends of the Bowery say and I was living in the Mex diggings with a pack of sheep men till my boss in New York wired me money. Now, old man, take some advice from a tough jay from back East . . . stay home and grow a mustache before you rush out into the red universe any more."

Then Crane took off into Mexico, and it was perfect. The mountain grandeur stirred his ingrained *Naturmystik*. The strange language and new culture sharpened his perceptions, deepened his sense of wonder, opened windows upon self-realization—provided him all the joys of the traveler. "Mexican Sights and Street Scenes," as he wrote them up for Bacheller, gave him to ironies about the suffering of burros, birds, and people in a gently callous, a calmly cruel society. The raffish international set in Mexico City was a joy. But the key adventure was altogether the real thing.

The principal record of this sojourn is the fine tale, "Horses— One Dash." There is simply no way, from what one knows of Crane's quite normal tendency to refocus events into literature, to tell what "really" happened. He went out with a local guide into the territory of Ramon Colorado, a small *bandido*; perhaps he went to interview a bandit for Bacheller, or to see what he could see, and Colorado found him first. The skeleton of the tale is that, when Crane and his guide took lodging in a sinister hamlet, a drunken, swaggering bandit and crew came in; and, just the other side of the doorway, they sat feasting, swilling, and bragging up their courage to burst in and rob the Americano of his money, revolver, and spurs. Crane knew the deepest physical fear of his personal life to date and the guide gibbered; but, just as the bandits seemed about to burst in, a bevy of local whores arrived and diverted them. Crane and the guide then sneaked out at daybreak and rode madly ahead of Colorado and crew until saved by a patrol of *rurales*. These events are the gist of the tale as he wrote it—and apparently as he told it with gusto before he wrote it.

The despatches to Bacheller were meanwhile keeping his memory alive at home. They appeared not as news but as features and often long after Crane had left Mexico. The *Philadelphia Press* on May 19, 1895, subheaded "Mexican Sights and Street Scenes" as "The Author of 'The Red Badge of Courage' in the Aztec Capital." And on July 21, "Ancient Capital of Montezuma / The Brilliant Author of 'The Black Riders' Describes a Trip." *The Black Riders* was announced for publication on May 11, 1895. It may have been that event, the climax of what was probably the happiest twelve-month's span in his life, which brought Crane back home in May.[13]

VIII

Fame, praise, and deference could be more dangerous than neglect and abuse, Crane was shortly to find, but not yet. The advent of *The Black Riders* discovered a fascinating fact about his fame: his contemporaries couldn't bear it, especially the newspaper boys. Serious criticism, which mostly came along in the fall, treated his revolution seriously. But the "paragraphers," paid to be clever, howled like the "Indians" in Vosburgh's studio. Crane seems to have understood their envy, their need to feel outraged and reach for corrective satire, the commercialism which inspired their cracks and epithets, and their scores of usually stupid parodies. "I was the mark for every humorist in the country," he remarked later—but he survived to write more verse. "Abuse and ridicule" hurt a man of dignity; but they were insignificant beside the allegiance of "men of sense":

Garland, Howells, and in this case, also Harry Thurston Peck, Barry, the reviewer for *The Nation,* and at last even *The Atlantic Monthly.*[14]

And Crane discovered shortly that a group of lesser "men of sense" around Bacheller not only thought him clubable but wished to make him the star of the Lantern Club, sometimes called in the *fin de siècle* mode "The Lanthorne." It was a shanty on a rooftop approachable only by an iron ladder. There was lunch every day, and Howells and Mark Twain each came. On Saturday nights stories were read on assignment, and nothing but dispraise was allowed. "The highest tribute that a story could receive was complete silence," Bacheller recalled. Not only close friends like Edward Marshall and Willis Hawkins belonged but also Richard Watson Gilder, who had found *Maggie* too tough for the *Century Magazine.*

Crane's summer was another good one, including a renewal of the grand Pike County picnic. He rode, hiked, and hunted out of Ed's new home in lovely Hartwood, New York. He began to write up Mexico, and started a novel about the Art Students' League Building "Indians" which became *The Third Violet.* And then the long-sought fame descended.

At first it did not look like nemesis. Appleton's published *The Red Badge of Courage* early in October, 1895, and the reviews were very good in spite of a few cavils in New York. Crane began to get·interested letters from editors as well as fans. Elbert Hubbard of *The Philistine* got up an elaborate testimonial dinner for the "cause" of Crane (and the greater glory of Fra Elbertus), and Willis Hawkins persuaded Steve to go—even supplying the dinner jacket and overcoat. And Crane had one moment of sheer, joyous triumph. As he wrote to Hawkins:

> The dinner scheme mingles my emotions. In one sense, it portends an Ordeal but in the larger sense it overwhelms me in pride and arrogance to think that I have such friends.
>
> By the way, you ought to see the effect of such things on my family. Ain't they swelled up, though! Gee! I simply can't go around and see 'em near enough. It's great. I am no longer a black sheep but a star.[15]

Obviously, even in this whoop of joy Crane's feelings are mingled. He has every reason to fear deflation, if from nothing else than self-ridicule. Life was still full of obstacles. He took his catboat out into the lake and sent it booming through a new part where sunken stumps, snags, and old logs gave it thump after shuddering thump. With each his anger rose till, all alone, he flew into screaming hysteria—the first time in his life he had ever completely lost his temper, he told Hawkins.

Perhaps that was therapeutic. The Philistine dinner, in Buffalo, New York, was attended not by celebrities but by old friends and newspaper people—more "Indians." They acted that way, but there is no evidence that Crane was upset. Frank W. Noxon, an old D. U., thought Crane was "having the time of his life" amid the uproar, and Crane told Miss Nellie Crouse as much when he used a documented account of the affair as bait to open a correspondence with her on New Year's Eve;[16] his object, possibly, was matrimony. Perhaps the ghost of Chatterton had been laid.

The Apprentice Sorcerer

ACTUALLY, of course, within four and a half years from New Year's Day, 1896, Crane would be on his deathbed in the Black Forest. 1896 might have been the year in which success stabilized his personal life and his professional career and set him firmly on the way of growth which could have matured his genius and conceivably set his achievement on the highest level. Instead, while the books and fame piled up, Crane's life moved from one disaster to another until by New Year's Day, 1897, he was, symbolically as well as actually, aboard the filibuster tug *Commodore* off the coast of Florida—sinking. He would burn out the year as he did his brief life in restless, desperate seeking—for the right woman, the right way of life, endurable relations with his celebrity; for truth, control of his art, command of his creative impulses—for something (who really knows what?) hidden away in his psyche. As Howells perceptively remarked, Crane sought "the secret of himself." He would remain a brilliant apprentice to his life and art.

Pretty obviously, no artist is "arrived" until he has mastered the problems of the materials, the way of treating them, and the reasons for treating them that way which will, altogether, permit his art. His creative impulses must be quickened and freed to bring to light the potentialities his technical skill can triumphantly convert. He may have successively and repeatedly to master such problems as he changes styles. But he must at least begin by serving whatever apprenticeship is necessary to his mastery. He must work, learn, produce, imitate, discard, struggle, and persevere until he is "in the secret of himself."

In another but allied sense, the same is true of being young and growing up. And of course young artists go through both processes more or less at once. A few of them, as they experiment, produce learner's work, "studio pieces," so absolutely brilliant as to constitute art strangely true, even great. Perhaps that applies to all the Chattertonians. No doubt it also does, for example, to the poetry of Milton through "Lycidas." And certainly it applies to the best of Stephen Crane. He never lived into the exact secret of himself. And no more shall we. The knowable secret of Stephen Crane is that in art, in life, in thought, he remained an experimenter, a seeker of rare, wonderful gifts, an apprentice sorcerer.

That it seems is the key to the interminable debates about whether Crane was realist, romanticist, neo-realist, naturalist, symbolist, impressionist, or what have you. He was any kind of an "—ist" available to him from the weather of his times because he was investigating, experimenting with it all and trying to find out just which best suited him. But he was not any of them, really, because he had not settled on any. He did an astonishing amount of brilliant work in various styles, from various viewpoints. He overpowered all by the force of his own imagination's way. But he did not live, unlike his contemporary, Joyce, for instance, to establish finally what that way was.

In spite of Hubbard's Philistines and all, Crane seems to have taken the first hubbub over *The Red Badge* pretty well. He had begun it as a pot-boiler, and he knew Howells thought *Maggie* and *George's Mother* better. He was sure he could improve on them all. He was habituated to "abuse" over *The Black Riders* and inclined to discount extremists. And then the wave of British adoration of *The Red Badge* swept in and smashed him right off his feet. Eventually the pressures of what critics were saying in London and of the reactions of people he knew threw Crane into something like panic.

It all came to a head with the publication on January 26, 1896, of the dispatch to the *New York Times* by its London correspondent, the American novelist Harold Frederic: "Stephen Crane's Triumph"—the kind of story every young writer dreams of meriting. The praise was unstinting for Crane's "unique grasp" of subject and his originality of "construction." Frederic guessed perceptively that the author had imagined, not participated in, war. Frederic understood *The Red Badge of Courage* more fully than any other reviewer and called it "one of the deathless books which must be read by everybody who desires

[46]

to be, or to seem, a connoisseur of fiction." He proclaimed that literary London rang with the name of Stephen Crane.

In dealing with Crane, one is forced inevitably to guess. And one good guess seems to be that word of Frederic's piece got around literary New York a few days before the Sunday *Times* printed it. At the Lantern Club, horse-play ceased while a solemn toast was drunk to Crane—and what he called "the social crisis" hit him. He could only "call them damned fools and sit down again."[1] In New York he became "a gibbering idiot," as he wrote Ripley Hitchcock.[2] ". . . Oh you don't know how that damned city tore my heart out by the roots and flung it under the heels of its noise," he apologized to Hawkins. ". . . On Friday it had me keyed to a point where I was no more than a wild beast and I had to make a dash willy-nilly."[3] He fled to the hills of Hartwood. Thence, on the day Frederic's piece would appear, he wrote Nellie Crouse and the next day Howells of a moving, almost tragic fear that success and praise would corrupt, delude, or swerve him from the paths of truth, honor, and courage. In a life always to be young, it was a moment of rare and profound self-penetration.

Such self-knowledge might help, as it did, with the morale of Crane's situation. It did not help with the key career problem—where to go from here? In a year's time his position as writer had been reversed. *The Black Riders* and *The Red Badge of Courage* had been published. This year *George's Mother* would appear. *Maggie* would be for the first time published (not merely printed). McClure would bring out *The Little Regiment* in his magazine and Appleton publish it between covers. Hubbard would do the tiny *A Souvenir and a Medley,* and *The Third Violet* would begin serialization and then emerge between covers the next year. Crane was now in hot demand with syndicate and magazine editors as well as publishers.

But all this writing came from his past. There remained the young writer's terrible problem of what to write about. Added was the agony following any first success: how to follow it up and keep the career running. Crane's sense of life as a battle became now a series of interlocking challenges to fights he was on the whole to lose. His problems were: how to manage his success; how to find the materials for a rise from rather than a mere continuation of that challenged and potentially evanescent success; more fundamentally, how to secure that vision, that method, that art-style which was also a life-style to see him through as theirs had the masters of the past.

I

Nothing came of going to Washington for McClure. And nothing but real trouble came from trying to hark back to the "Midnight Sketches" idea and muckrake the police of New York. Not even friendship with Police Commissioner Theodore Roosevelt saved Crane from a real debacle there. Apparently it had not occurred to Crane, used in his heart to total obscurity, that he was ripe to be framed. But he was. His fame rested largely on sensation: what was to the Victorian American mind the blasphemy of *The Black Riders,* the febrile garishness of his style, the dirtiness of *Maggie: A Girl of the Streets,* the grimy pessimism of *George's Mother,* the Bohemianism of *The Third Violet.*

The century-long tradition of romantic reputation, founded luridly on Byron, DeQuincey, Poe, seemed to apply perfectly to Stephen Crane. And there was no dearth of volunteers to plaster it on him. Thomas Beer calls his chapter on this period "Fame and Prejudice." Wholly false gossip about Crane's drunkenness and opium addiction were assiduously spread; and then, of course, since he had neither home nor wife and was a notorious Bowery haunter, women (Byron's vice). Obviously, to the Victorian mind, the author of *Maggie* must have been addicted to whores. Obviously also, in the tradition he was vulnerable to seduction stories. Semi-professional Crane-baiters had New York ringing with such tales in 1896.[4]

And at least on the question of women, Crane handed them devastating ammunition. It is, in fact, impossible yet to know how much fire there was beneath the smoke. Much of the testimony of witnesses who could have known about Crane is contradictory. The surviving evidence lends itself to ambiguity of interpretation. One reads it one way if he commits himself to the faith that Crane was "guilty"—of promiscuity, of commercial vice. He reads it another if he decides that Crane was quixotic about women as about many things. Beer—like Crane's friends Linson, Noxon, and Gordon—was convinced of Crane's essential "innocence." Stallman, Gilkes, and Zara, like Crane's friend Hilliard, are convinced of his "guilt." Berryman, who is accepted by Hoffman, has a lay-Freudian notion of Crane as a special case.

Everybody might agree, however, that the whole question is complicated by Crane's life-long preacher's kid's defiance of moralism—the *méfiance* which made him exult in the appearance of evil. Not only did he refuse to protect his reputation, he deliberately, publicly courted as a celebrity about New York the disapprobation he had been trained to avoid at all costs in childhood and had rebelliously sought since early adolescence in Asbury Park. Finally, as his defeated courtship of Miss Nellie Crouse of Akron, Ohio, suggests, Crane in his twenty-fifth year showed signs of matrimonial inclination. It does not seem to have struck him that women, especially of a certain age, might feel the same about him. The net result was some kind of "involvement" with four disturbed, if not disreputable, women in 1896.

The fourth of these eventually became "Mrs. Stephen Crane," but there is no evidence to convince any judicious observer that Crane was either in love with any of the other three, or in bed with any of them. The first was, according to Beer, Doris Watts of various aliases. Crane let her touch him for various loans, and she seems to have tried to blackmail him, perhaps into marriage. When Crane finally came to call her off, she hurled a knife from her "Turkish Corner" which nearly impaled him. The story reverberated across New York.

Then came Dora Clark in a case one might guess that Crane deliberately manufactured. Perhaps not, but some of the facts tempt one to such an interpretation. Crane had been avowedly studying the massively corrupt New York police. He had been in touch with Theodore Roosevelt, the new commissioner whose clean-up program the "Force" was energetically resisting. He sat on the bench with Magistrate Brown of the Jefferson Market Court all day on September 16, 1896. That night he sat in the Broadway Garden with a couple of chorus girls until they were joined by Dora Clark—who knew one of the girls but not Crane. Dora, twenty and pretty, was not an ordinary girl-about-town. She had a recent and very active police record, having been picked up on sight by plainclothes men "half a dozen times in five weeks." She believed herself—and reporters for the *Times* and *World,* at least, reflected her belief—to be the victim of organized police persecution for having turned the laugh on a detective in court, with a racial slur.

Was it accident that Crane was introduced to her? Or that he took all three girls out on the corner and left Dora Clark talking to one girl while he put the third on a street car—all in sight of a plainclothes man whom Dora Clark apparently knew was standing across the street? The policeman, Becker, much later electrocuted for an extortion-murder, arrested Dora Clark for soliciting and tried to run Crane and the other girl out of the picture by threats. When it didn't work, he took them all to the station. The other girl, unfortunately for Crane, went into howling hysterics. Dora Clark was locked up. The police sergeant tried to talk Crane out of wrecking his reputation by appearing in the case. Next day the New York papers carried flash accounts of Stephen Crane's appearance before Magistrate Brown to save a persecuted girl from a false charge of soliciting

The stories were, contrary to tradition, uniformly admiring of Crane, anti-police, and pro-Dora. The least factual and most fiction-like (though devoid of the obvious tags of his style) appeared in the *Journal* and may have been written by Crane himself.[5] It is by no means impossible that Crane, the reporters, and the girls had set a trap designed to protect Dora Clark, to expose and so help reform the police, and to pay short-run journalistic and long-run literary dividends to the writers. Whether that is so or not, the affair in the end was a disaster.

In spite of good newspaper protection, the affair spattered pitch on Crane that wouldn't come off. As late as the next January, papers in New England, Rochester, even Nashville jeered at the Crane whom the New York papers and the syndicates made a hero after the *Commodore* sinking. "The owners of the 'Commodore' as well as Dora Clark, must come to the conclusion that Stephen Crane is a Jonah," said the *Rochester Herald* on January 7. And the *Boston Advertiser* concurred on the 9th: "Novelist Crane is now in a position to tell us which he regards as the most dangerous way to get material for a realistic romance, seeing the elephant in the Tenderloin or enlisting on a filibustering Cuban expedition."[6] They represented many others.

In spite of public promises from magistrates, the New York

police no more stopped persecuting Dora Clark then they reformed for Roosevelt. They simply put Stephen Crane on the harassment list. And that may have made him seem the more vulnerable to a middle-aged, widowed, ex-actress, Amy Leslie, who worked as drama critic for the *Chicago News*. She had been an admirer of Crane and later claimed to have loaned him (or given him for deposit) $800.00. The facts are obscure. Crane gave Hawkins money for her, and for a long time he remained solicitous of her mental balance and was careful to remit money until she quarrelled with Hawkins and eventually sued Crane. The *Chicago News* became one of the most flagrant and persistent of Crane-haters.

II

Whether or not Crane's New York affairs represented lust in action, they certainly cost a waste of spirit and an expense of shame. They were disastrous to Crane's personal life and evidently wholly frustrating to his imagination. He got no literature out of any of them, except perhaps hints toward the absurd *femme fatale* of *Active Service*. He was little in advance of his condition at Claverack while reporting Harvard football games during that fall, 1896. But actually his situation was less desperate—or, from another point of view, more so—than it seemed. What should have been the normal context of New York had become chaos, development wholly blocked. He was waiting around town for orders "to ship" on a cloak-and-dagger filibustering expedition which he would report from rebellion-torn Cuba. He would see war at first hand.

Sometime early in November he got his contract, put $700.00 in Bacheller's gold in a moneybelt, and took off for Jacksonville on the next train, too suddenly to tell anybody. There was journalistic logic in that for Bacheller; there was perhaps artistic as well as adventurous logic for Crane (who had just turned twenty-five). It has often been suspected that there was also a deep, hidden logic in it for a psyche looking for death—but who can really say? For the physical Crane the situation presently settled into ordinary military logic: he had hurried, now he waited.

While he waited, he met the climactic one of 1896's strange

ladies. And, *pace* Berryman, she was very little like the others—
or like anyone else he had ever known, except that she was a
gallant, out-and-out rebel like himself. Cora Howorth Murphy
Stewart, alias Taylor, had come a long and battered way from
her mildly esthetic, prosperous, and certainly respectable Boston
family. The informed conjectures of her biographer, Miss Lillian
Gilkes, a tireless researcher, show Cora revolting against Boston;
marrying and divorcing Murphy in New York; marrying Captain
Donald Stewart, a much decorated soldier of Victoria's Empire,
in London; leaving Stewart when he set forth upon overseas
colonial service; and arriving at last (perhaps dumped from
a junketing millionaire's yacht, who knows?) in Jacksonville.
There she had gone into business on the "nice" edge of the
underworld. She was mistress of the "Hotel de Dream," a night-
club with a local "class-A rating" as one "of the better houses of
ill-fame."[7]

If, as Miss Gilkes argues, Cora was "technically" not a madam
because her girls did not actually live there, hers was certainly
at best a house of assignation and Mrs. Taylor was making a
capitalist's success from the conduct of a "disorderly house."
But there is no evidence that that was what especially attracted
Stephen Crane. He had a long wait in Jacksonville, and it was
there Charles Michelson observed Crane's skill in stalking sailors
and wharf-rats in waterfront dives. What with the publication
of *Maggie* and his strange experiences with women and gossip,
he may also have decided to "see" prostitution as he had hoped
to see war. He later presented a different, full-fledged madam
"on the line" an autographed copy of *Maggie*.[8]

But not even that would explain his fascination with Cora
Taylor. In all his rather feeble writing about women, it seems
clear that their Victorian games of irrational emotionality alternating with rigid convention simply suffocated Crane. It was
one thing he never began to see through. In Cora, however, he
found a woman of taste, intelligence, vitality, some good looks,
who was incapable of playing the hypocritical games of respectability on him. It was not only that she was strategically mis-
placed for that; she was also intellectually and spiritually in revolt
against it; and she conducted her person and her life with the
integrity of courageous choice, as Miss Gilkes makes clear. Con-
ventionally she was a lady *manquée* as Crane was a gentleman

manqué. Of course it must have seemed, as serious love always seems, a matter of destiny when Cora fell frankly in love with him as he came to the "Hotel de Dream" while going "down the line."

Parenthetically, it may be useful to comment that Cora was not merely personally "aloof," like madams generally, from the main business conducted in her house. She was operating a "class" establishment; and her sophistication, poise, and charm provided the class. These characteristics surely were essential conditions for Crane's interest in her. Vice versa, it is difficult to suppose that, had Crane simply come rollicking through, paying his money and having his girl, Cora would have been smitten by him. Much more likely, he intrigued her in his natural role of the searcher into life for art.

The erstwhile preacher's kid, the temperamental (and now professional) watcher and self-watcher, must early have been roused to irony deeper than usual by the discovery that Captain Stewart was not only alive but vindictive: he would grant no divorce. It did not help with any of Crane's problems to discover that he could perhaps never regularly marry Cora. In the light of his reputation, what would become of them both if they were linked publicly? No expression of his love for Cora is happy, and the most lyric sounds like a farewell: "To C.P.S. / Love comes like the tall swift shadow of a ship at night. . . . Then silence and a bitter silence—the silence of the sea at night."[9]

III

Meanwhile there was the business for which he was carrying Bacheller's gold-pieces and upon which he staked still more precious hopes for his career. The business of filibustering (in this case sneaking munitions to the Cuban rebels), consisted largely, as a reporter colleague of Crane's recalled, in lurking. Dark, foggy conspiring wasted the weeks until at length on New Year's Day, 1897, the tug *Commodore* got her guns and ammunition stowed and left, amid rebel songs and muttered Spanish threats, for a little beachhead. At once there were hints of disorganization and sabotage. Water flooded the engine room the second night for no apparent reason, the pumps failed, and she sank about dawn of January 2.

The event was dangerous, exhausting, painful, shocking, but not heroic. Experience once more dealt Crane bathos and disillusion for his hopes. As might have been expected, there was chaos on the sinking *Commodore* and things got worse at the end. Signed aboard as able seaman at $20.00 per month as an official blind, Crane worked himself almost to collapse bailing in the hellish engine room and straining to get boats launched. Off himself in the last and littlest one—a ten-foot dinghy with four or possibly five men in it—he had to watch the drowning of the seven-man crew of the first mate's boat which apparently foundered at the ship's side. Possibly what happened was the drowning of three and the desertion of four others on a raft after the ship sank—or possibly the raft was sucked down by the drowning *Commodore.*

Then came the trip—of ten, twelve, fifteen, twenty miles (the distance is in dispute)—across more or less dangerous waves (the degree is in dispute).[10] It was a long, slow affair, perhaps much too-long delayed by the crippled, mournful captain, who decided to lie offshore all the night rather than go in at dusk. When exhausted they did go in, Billy Higgins, the oiler, the best man in the boat, was meaninglessly killed in the surf.

Largely because Crane was in it, the *Commodore's* filibuster had aspects of a publicity circus from the start. On the day she sailed, the New York *Press*, part of Bacheller's syndicate, not only announced it but listed essential items of cargo: 200,000 rifle cartridges, 1,000 Hotchkiss rounds, 2,000 dynamite cartridges, 1,000 pounds of dynamite, and "Stephen Crane, the novelist." On January 3, the *Press* screamed "Filibuster Sunk . . . Stephen Crane Missing," and word of his death flashed round the world. Next day the headlines read: "More of the Filibusters Safe/ Commodore's Wrecked Seamen Struggle for Life in a Heavy Surf / Stephen Crane, Novelist, Swims Ashore / Young New York Writer Astonishes the Sea Dogs by His Courage in the Face of Death." The cook was quoted as saying not only that the "newspaper feller was a nervey man" but that Crane had rescued a fifth seaman from the dinghy (one never mentioned by Crane) and had himself been rescued by broken-armed Captain Murphy. It was not until January 7 that the *Press* had "Stephen Crane's Own Story."

In Crane's "own story" he presented himself only as observer and Murphy and Higgins as heroes. His report said almost nothing about the hours in the dinghy. It is usual and probably correct to suppose that he held off because his imagination was already germinating its one true gain from all that agony. "The Open Boat," written in Jacksonville during the next couple of months, is one of the triumphs of Crane's creativity. It is one of the great tales of this period he was now fatally entering— one which produced some of the world's great short stories but negligible novels.

The incident of the shipwreck is forever important because "The Open Boat" grew from it. But it was important also that the whole experience was deeply frustrating to Crane. He was loyal to Captain Murphy. And, yet, there were those seven marooned on and by the *Commodore*: in the first mate's plunge to death Crane had seen "rage, rage, rage unspeakable. . . ." And there was the loss of Billy Higgins. Had Murphy been treacherous, weak, mistaken, or merely trapped by mischance?

Crane never openly speculated. With Bacheller's gold at the bottom of the sea, Crane staggered "home" to Cora's frantic arms. He scraped together what money he could and slogged for weeks through Florida swamps trying to elude a *Commodore*-embarrassed United States Navy and failing. His family always thought his health was permanently wrecked in Florida. Defeated and more desperate than ever, he gave up in March and negotiated a contract with William Randolph Hearst to report on the incipient Greco-Turkish War. He began to announce that he had to see if *The Red Badge* really was right about war. Before he left Jacksonville it was apparently arranged that Cora Taylor would sell out and follow him to London and on to Greece, there to become "Imogene Carter," first woman war correspondent. He talked to Linson in New York about how to arrange a marriage without subjecting his affianced to the "weasels" of gossip. Then he sailed, never to "live" in the United States again.

IV

Nor is it clear that in any full sense he lived anywhere. Henceforth it was much a matter of conscious life in death, of a surviving which could not be long, must often be painful and only seldom, in his work, significant.

There was so much building up to awful letdowns. In London he tasted his fame as only Londoners and Americans there knew how to serve it up to a visiting lion. Harold Frederic squired him around, and Richard Harding Davis took him into the brotherhood by giving a luncheon to meet J. M. Barrie, Justin McCarthy, and Anthony Hope. Heineman the publisher loaded him with compliments and got him a contract to write correspondence for the *Westminster Gazette*. Going down to Dover, Frederic and Crane were joined by Davis, a fabulous all-American boy type. On the docks Davis saw "Lady Stewart" with Crane and, according to Miss Gilkes, recognized Cora Taylor of the "Hotel de Dream"—and froze.

Nevertheless Crane and "Imogene Carter" with her long-time companion, Mrs. Ruedy, went on to the war, touristing as they went. The war, when they got there, was swiftly a fiasco. Crane started out pro-Greek and most optimistic about what "these people of the mountains" would do in their "people's war." But the war declared on April 17 was ended in Greek humiliation by May 20, and Crane had only a brief chance to view combat (at a distance) with tragic exultation and to bleed psychically for refugees and betrayed soldiers. He got off at least thirteen dispatches,[11] however, including two which were among his very best writing. They match Hemingway at his own game. Hearst's *Journal* headlined them flamboyantly: "That Was the Romance, 'The Red Badge of Courage'—a Story. This Is the Reality, a Battle Today in Greece—a Fact. By Stephen Crane"; and "My Talk With Soldiers Six."

He came out feeling that *The Red Badge* was all right. He did not see much in this war which his imagination had not told him, though his best writing about it is peculiarly conscious of variant possibilities in point of view. For he wrote:

> The roll of musketry fire was tremendous. In the distance it sounded like the tearing of a cloth. Nearer it sounded like rain on a resonant roofing, and close by it was just long crash after crash. It was a beautiful sound; beautiful as had never been dreamed. It was more impressive than the roar of Niagara and finer than thunder or an avalanche, because it had the wonder of human tragedy in it. It was the most beautiful sound of my experience, barring no symphony. The crash of it was ideal.

This is from one point of view. The other might be taken

from the men who died there. The slaughter of Turks was great, . . . the insane and almost wicked squadrons were practically annihilated, and their scattered fragments slid slowly back, leaving the plain black with wounded and dead men and horses.

From a distance it was like a game. No blood, no expressions of horror were to be seen; there were simply the movements of tiny doll tragedy.[12]

Or again:

. . . And this quality provided the picture with its extraordinary mysticism. These little black things streaming from here and there on the plain, what were they? What moved them to this? The power and majesty of this approach was all in its . . . inexplicable mystery. What was this thing? and Why was it? Of course—Turks—Turks—Turks, but then that is a mere name used to describe these creatures who were really hobgoblins and endowed with hobgoblin motives. In the olden times one could have had a certain advantage of seeing an enemy's eyes. If one was anxious about the battle one could have perhaps witnessed the anxiety of the enemy. Anything is better than a fight with an army that wears a black velvet mask of distance. . . . And now began the infantry fight at the foot of the height. . . . The whole of this sharp, hard attack was incoherent, and the strength of the drama of it was in this incoherence. . . . The Turks did not come like a flood, nor did the Greeks stand like adamant. It was simply a shifting, changing, bitter, furious struggle, where one could not place odds nor know when to run.[13]

The actual experience in Greece of love and war taught Crane more of what Henry James meant by "point of view" and what Howells meant by "complicity." In the ultimate failure of his Greek War novel, *Active Service,* his sole artistic gain was, once more, a triumph in the short story, "Death and the Child." And in it are notes new to his fiction which Cora on her side and the foreign soldiers on the other had given him. In the presence of the real thing, the tale's hero is "edified, aghast, triumphant . . . he remembered the pageants of carnage that had marched through the dreams of his childhood. Love he knew; that he had confronted alone, isolated, wondering, an individual, an atom taking the hand of a titanic principle. Like the faintest breeze on his forehead, he felt here the vibration from the hearts of 40,000 men." But he had somewhere also heard something which filled in a gap in the sense of combat in all his previous war writing: it had always lacked the essential feel for the real presence of the missile. But now the nearby soldiers know that the bolting protagonist has not been wounded: "Otherwise they would have heard the silken, sliding, tender noise of the bullet, and the thud of its impact."[14]

Amid the clamor of glamor at home, however, such subtle realities went unappreciated. As a Hearst man, Crane became more than ever fair game. Davis had created the role of the fabulous foreign correspondent, and Hearst blew Crane up to the same proportions. Crane continued, of course, to register his responses to events, and that led to a much lampooned overemphasis on personal pronoun "I", especially when he crammed correspondence into form for overseas cabling. The later, full-scale stories were far more objective and dramatic. And, of course, Hearst exploited Crane's name and personality all he could. Another Hearst man in Greece, set to observe Crane observing, painted himself in a slit-trench cautiously studying "the pale, thin face of the novelist as the latter seated himself on an ammunition box amid a shower of shells and casually lighted a cigarette."[15]

Of course there were howls of rage and delight from every paragraphing Crane-baiter in America, and these were now augmented by the enthusiastic enemies of Hearst. They rushed into lampoon and parody. An unknown bard from Lewiston, Maine, immortalized himself with a Crane war-dispatch poem:

> I have seen a battle.
> I find it very like what
> I wrote up before.
> I congratulate myself that
> I ever saw a battle.
> I am pleased with the sound of war.
> I think it is beautiful.
> I thought it would be.
> I am sure of my nose for battle.
> I did not see any war correspondents while
> I was watching the battle except
> I.[16]

But the *Denver Post* was niftiest of all on May 20 when its paragrapher reported: "It is said that before leaving Greece, General Miles will see everything that is to be seen at the seat of war. It will be quite an imposing spectacle when Richard Harding Davis and Stephen Crane pass before him in review."

With the country ringing with that sort of thing and New York with slander far worse, and after the encounter with Davis had made it quite clear what could happen to (and because of) Cora, it was obvious that there could be no return home. England seemed the obvious answer in spite of the far-distant Captain Stewart. There Crane's professional relations were cordial, his reputation enviable, and no newspaper or police-war raged against him. And there, at least among Fourth Estate people, sexual taboos were loosening. Harold Frederic bigamously kept American wives in two establishments.[17] Other writers and artists, among them H. G. Wells, lived comfortably without matrimonial bonds. By early June Stephen and Cora, with a crazy retinue consisting of Mrs. Ruedy, twin Greek refugees, and a Greek puppy, had settled into "Ravensbrook Villa," Oxted, Surrey.[18] All Crane had to do was support them with his pen.

V

His had never been a commercially ready pen. Creatively, Crane was facile only when the agony of getting something "filtered" through his blood was done. He was far in maturity, experience, and achieved self-discovery from the reliable fecundity of masters like James and Howells who could turn out a novel a year and have time over for minor enterprises. And, of course, Greece had no more cured his crisis than Florida.

Neither could Cora help him, though she loved him dearly and doubtless did everything in her power. A minor but terribly damaging fact was that it was not in her power to economize. She seems to have been as improvident of outgo as Crane. The only obvious explanation for her relative business success before and after Crane's appearance in her life is that she was in a business in which money traditionally flows free and easy and spending is requisite to success.

Otherwise, as a marriage (official or not), their domesticity at first went beautifully—even for Crane's writing. Of course, it was convenient, perhaps mandatory, that Cora become for the neighborhood and for new friends "Mrs. Crane." Stephen went so far as to write an earlier friend, Sanford Bennett, that he had been married in Paris about August 24. Possibly he had. There was not much reason why Cora should have taken bigamy more seriously then Frederic. But it seems more likely that Miss Gilkes is right in maintaining that there was never a formal, *de jure* marriage.

In this period, drawing magnificently on his slim capital both for materials and for psychic energy, Crane wrote a series of his finest short pieces. In spite of a month out to recuperate from a carriage accident, he produced, between June and the following February in about the following order, "The Monster," drawing on Port Jervis; and his best Western tales: "The Bride Comes to Yellow Sky," "Five White Mice," and "The Blue Hotel." He banked his Greek dividend, "Death and the Child," but he failed to do much with *Active Service* despite Frederic's command. Small wonder he was exhausted at the end—and wild at his complicated failure to succeed financially with work of that quality. In the whole period he got no unborrowed money from the States: Amy Leslie had his Appleton's royalties blocked, and his new things sold slowly.

Crane could not care for the holders of current English literary reputations. Swinburne bored him even worse than Henry James —who was at least resolutely kind; and George Meredith snubbed him. Crane in turn alienated both wings of the going British neo-romanticism. Like Howells, Crane had no use for the late, extravagantly lamented Stevenson. "I believe in ghosts," he said. "Mr. Stevenson has not passed away far enough. He is all around town." Neither could he care for the *fin de siècle fleurs du mal*. Except Yeats, everybody talked about Oscar Wilde "like a lot of little girls at a Sunday School party when a kid says a wicked word in a corner," said the Reverend Crane's son. "Wilde was a mildewed chump. He has a disease and they all gas about him as though there was a hell and he came up out of it,"[19] said the close student of the Bowery. Instead of panic, the literary social occasion now moved him to scorn.

His English friends at this stage were, naturally enough, either other foreigners like Joseph Conrad or, as in New York, bohemian "Indians"—like Frederic, who was both. The London

"Indians" were chummy and fun. But "Indian"-like, they never knew when to stop. They blew in at random, consuming and exhausting Cora's lavish hospitality and Crane's too thin energies. The confluence of pressures made him dream again of escape—to the Klondike, to the Sudan, to someplace exotic where perhaps he might yet find himself and his way.

On February 15 the *Maine* was blown up in Havana harbor, and the U. S. government began the deadly little minuet which announced nineteenth-century wars. England, like all Europe, stirred with antagonism at the crass arrogance of the Yankees and was assured that, if there were a war, proud Castile would slap the Yankees down. On April 11 McKinley sent the message one step short of open war to Congress, and on April 13 the House and on the sixteenth the Senate passed confirming resolutions. On the twenty-fifth McKinley declared war. Sometime before the declaration Crane had become convinced that war—the real thing this time—was certain. Desperately he begged and borrowed money and shot off to New York to join the Navy.

VI

It may have been at the naval recruitment office which rejected him that Crane learned that he was the victim of active pulmonary tuberculosis.[20] If so, neither that fact nor the rejection sent him home. He knew another way to get to the war. He went around to the *World* and took Pulitzer's shilling to go as a correspondent. After hanging around New York long enough to learn that it was an established fact that he was a dope addict, he left for Key West and the waiting, "phony" part of the war—by far the worst for a word-man. And there, amid the hordes of other correspondents, Crane discovered the impossibility of his situation. His celebrity was compounded of three contrary factors, and he was temperamentally and habitually fitted to perform publicly the role of only the falsest one. There was his literary fame—which no man ever could portray except on the pages of his art. There was his largely accidental image of glamorous correspondent, a role in the Davis mode which he necessarily refused even to approximate. And there was his notoriety as romantic satanist—a role he had elaborately played since boyhood.

Consequently he projected an image enthusiastically hated and envied by all but understanding old friends. Charles Michelson, one of them, records inimitably the wracked, sunken body, the reserved but daring psyche—who got himself dubbed "Lord Tholepin" after rumors of an English manor house drifted back:

> Crane on his way to war was one of the most unprepossessing figures that ever served as a nucleus for apocryphal romances, shambling, with hair too long, usually lacking a shave, dressed like any of the deck hands, hollow-cheeked, sallow, destitute of small talk, critical if not fastidious, marked with ill-health—the very antithesis of the conquering male.[21]

In the face of the quiet soldiers and sailors Crane felt ashamed of self-important journalists. But he dug hard, too, for news where there was none, and he recorded "Jackies" saying proudly, "We've got a hot ship—a hot ship."[22] When he did finally go ashore with the Marines at Caimanera, Guatanamo Bay, however, it was the real thing—and the first American action on Cuban soil.

The steady, abrasive tension of real fear and the exhaustion of war in a tropical climate suddenly became as real as the immediate presence of people who shot real bullets at other people and deliberately killed them. With a normal tinge of modern guilt, Crane saw normally that, in one aspect, it was very like sport—and the greatest show on earth. From another point of view, there was an agony to the actual deaths far more horrifying than anything he had imagined for readers.

Beer and Berryman have accepted stories that Crane "hallucinated" under the pressure and began to see things that were not there. This condition is made doubtful by the profound accuracy with which he registered and reported what happened. Of Marines getting ready to jump off into the brush on their first patrol to destroy a well from which night-fighters had been harassing them, Crane wrote, for example:

> One could note the prevalance of a curious expression—something dreamy, the symbol of minds striving to tear away the screen of the future and perhaps expose the ambush of death. It is not fear in the least [but] . . . wonder. . . . Little absurd indications of time, redolent of coffee, steak, porridge,

or . . . emblems of the departure of trains for Yonkers . . .
now were sinister, sombre with the shadows of . . . foreseen,
inexorable, invincible tragedy.

There was expert imagery, not hallucination, in the notion
that Mauser bullets flew so thick about the ridge that it seemed
a good player might have bagged a lot with a lacrosse stick.
Nor was there hallucination in the notion that trapping guerillas
in a thicket, flushing them out with shells from the supporting
warship, and then shooting them down against the hillside as they
broke cover in coveys was "like a grim and frightful field sport"
—any more than it was hallucinatory to call the famous World
War II naval victory the "Marianas Turkeyshoot." It was only
that Crane at last was there,[23] really seeing combat.

Typically, the already invalid Crane went all out physically
with the Marines, and he may have been in bad enough shape
when other correspondents rescued him. But there was no stop-
ping him. He picked up malaria to go with his tuberculosis and
pushed along, disregarding the way quinine wracked a stomach
long tender and an intestine apparently also tubercular. Eventually he was living on coffee, cigarettes, alcohol, and fruit. And
still he pushed himself harder, carrying water to fighting men,
tending the wounded, racing up jungly trails behind troops,
exhausting himself, then staggering back miles to try to file
his stories. This happened repeatedly on the days marked by the
Army landing at Daiquiri on June 22, then Las Guasimas, El
Caney, and San Juan Hill before the surrender of Santiago on
July 14. By the end of it, Crane was even more a wreck than the
Army riddled by yellow fever.

Did he try to get himself killed? Probably. One can make
all kinds of guesses why, though no explanation will ever be
better than a mere guess. But there seems small room for doubt
about the fact of his spectacular self-neglect in the face of his
multiple diseases, all of which did kill him fairly soon, though
not in Cuba. Further, there are the reports of his repeatedly
exposing himself to sniper fire—with the Marines and again with
the Rough Riders. Davis' account of the Rough Riders incident
is most revealing. Where the men were entrenching behind a
ridge, Crane exposed himself in a long, white raincoat, drawing
showers of bullets on the area. He ignored Col. Leonard Wood's

orders to get down, wandered around smoking his pipe, and was infuriatingly careless until Davis thought of the answer:

> I knew that to Crane, anything that savored of a pose was hateful, so . . . I called, "You're not impressing anyone by doing that, Crane." As I hoped he would, he instantly dropped to his knees. When he crawled over to where we lay, I explained, "I knew that would fetch you," and he grinned, and said, "Oh, was that it?"[24]

By July 7, Crane had collapsed into delirium and was ordered evacuated by his chief. Aboard a transport the only medical attention he got was the hysterically arrogant command of a surgeon that Crane quarantine himself for yellow fever. Crewmen smuggled him stewed tomatoes. So his magnificent account, "Stephen Crane's Vivid Story of the Battle of San Juan," was datelined "In Front of Santiago, July 4, via Old Point Comfort, Va., July 13." There he watched the fascinating spectacle of genteel vacationers receiving home their country's wounded, sick, and shattered. Then he visited the *World* office and found himself in effect fired. He had filed at least nineteen stories for the *World,* some of them the best of the war. But the office commandos were frosty. Perhaps they could not forgive him for being with the Army when Sampson smashed Cervera's fleet, or for filing Edward Marshall's story for Hearst when Ed was wounded, or for conducting campaigns against the crime of arming Americans with black powder when the Spaniards had smokeless, or for lambasting the nation's Press for giving all the glory to "Reginald Marmaduke Maurice Montmorenci Sturdevant" and ignoring the Regular Army's unknown "Michael Nolan," old professional.

Perhaps they could not forgive him for being Stephen Crane. It is imaginable that they were trying to be merciful to his tortured body. In any case, he quietly went back to Hearst. And after staying around New York long enough to collect the latest slanders (and perhaps to go to be checked by Dr. Trudeau, the famous lung man in the Adirondacks), he slipped away to see if there might not be more war in Puerto Rico. There was not, and not much real experience, though he tried "occupying" parts of the island just ahead of the American advance. Finally he slipped into Havana before it had been officially surrendered, where he was possibly liable to vengeance from the Havana police; and he knew again, for the first time since publication of *The Red Badge*, the dangerous, blessed relief of being underground.

Being so was apparently such a relief that he moved out of his hotel into an obscure boardinghouse and simply stopped communicating with anybody but the *New York Journal*, to which he sent sketches of life in Havana. Through most of September he apparently neither wrote nor picked up letters. He was reported "missing" in the papers. And missing he was—from all responsibility except to himself. Of course Cora, marooned high and dry financially as well as emotionally, became frantic. She stirred up everyone she could think of—the Crane family (with the jolt of their first news that Stephen had a "wife"); Hearst; English friends and publishers; and the United States government. Slowly, and with evident reluctance, Crane rose again to the surface.

Why? What had been going on in Havana? Not having died, Crane may have been attempting to gather his forces to live. He may have embarked on the first self-designed regimen of his life to try to restore his squandered strength. He may have been playing for time to think things out—it seems clear that he returned to England (and even, perhaps, to Cora) with great reluctance up to the final moment. Very oddly, he sailed at the end from New York to England by way of Havana. Was there another woman, as Cora intuitively feared? Or was Crane tempted to take a Rimbaudian exit from life, as Joseph Conrad's pessimism about his return suggests Conrad guessed?

The solid and impressive fact about the whole episode is that, in the midst of his formal feeling after great pain, Crane found his imaginative vitality restored and released. He was writing steadily and with great enthusiasm. He was producing short stories, poetry, and eye-witness war pieces. And his New York literary agent, Reynolds, was bombarded not only with them but with appeals to turn them quickly into lots of cash. What Crane was doing with his cash and what he intended to do with what Reynolds was to raise simply does not appear. Cora was certainly not getting it, and it was only her eventual success in raising money in England and seeing to it that Crane got it which pried him out of Havana. Then he went to New York.

There his situation was strangely mixed. He was a kind of war hero, having been mentioned in dispatches by the Marines for bravery under fire as a volunteer signalman near Guantanamo. And Davis had published his judgment that Crane was the best of the Cuban war correspondents. Relations with publishers were easy. *The Open Boat and Other Stories* had appeared just as he started for Cuba, with an extra section of "Midnight Sketches" in the English edition. *War Is Kind*, a second volume of verse, was accepted, and publishers bid for the forthcoming *Active Service*. Old friends were faithful, Howells cordial as ever; and such new friends as James Huneker and the great painter Albert Pinkham Ryder swam into his ken. He thought of getting a country house, or a Texas ranch, and "duelled" with Cora across the Atlantic to get her back.

Maybe a Poconos house or a Rio Grande ranch would have worked—or maybe nothing would have worked. It was obvious, at least in retrospect, that the mark of death was on Crane. Howells, who knew it well at first hand, saw his malaria. Crane slept endlessly and dawdled listlessly when not forcing himself to simulate vigor. And that, too, helped his enemies. Davis had to thrash a big photographer, Thomas Macumber, for clamoring that Crane was dying of syphilis. And the word went out among the police, where Becker was entrenching as perhaps the first American underworld czar, to "get" Crane. Friends barely saved him twice from false arrest, from blatant "frame-ups."

Cora had prepared a *fin de siècle* nest for them in an ancient, ruined manor house, hopefully "Indian"-proof, "Brede Place" in England. If Becker and Macumber convinced Crane that there was no place for him in New York, if Cora could not play the game of hope in Texas, he could turn to the "home" he had never seen at "Brede." If nothing better, presumably it would do to die in. He wandered off to Jacksonville and Havana and eventually took ship.

VII

There has been a great deal of controversy about "Brede." Was it a sensible place for Crane? Obviously not: Albuquerque or Colorado Springs or Lake Placid might have been much better, or "Ed's house" at Hartwood once more—or, at worst, if it had to be England, a snug flat with Cora and one servant. But that implied "taking care" of things and oneself, and neither Crane nor Cora was good at that. Left to himself, Crane thought broken-down historical "Brede" was pretty funny—but if Cora liked to be neo-romantic he was not going to disturb that any more than he did the conviction that he was all right and that he just needed a little motherly discipline to shape him into a machine producing saleable manuscript to pay off the bills.

Crane concealed his illness as long as he could. No torture could have induced him to explain that he was an artist or that artists have troubles not available to medicines of the will. He shouldered the incredible tangle of debts and "arrangements" awaiting him in England and did his best to write like a machine and meet current expenses, pay off debts, and perhaps provide something for Cora's future. He turned out a lot—with surprising gems in it like *The Whilomville Stories,* and "The Upturned Face."

But creative growth was at an end. He got involved in a good deal of meaninglessness like finishing *Active Service,* trying to write a Stevensonian romance to sell and still keep his integrity by kidding it in *The O'Ruddy,* or working on *Great Battles of the World.* He put merciless pressure on himself and on his agents, especially Pinker in London, and on publishers. He finally even achieved the mere pot-boiler in a good many of those last, desperate tales on which he toiled his life away at "Brede." Not, of course, that he was unwilling. He was living out the triple vision of his own irony. He was going to die anyway, wasn't he?

Naturally there was, as witnesses have protested, plenty of fun at "Brede." Crane would have held his courage in contempt if there hadn't been. "Indians" were necessary to him, and they were soon invited down to "Brede" along with palefaces like Henry James, H. G. Wells, Ford Madox [Hueffer] Ford, and Conrad. At Christmas there was a last, big, wonderful party at "Brede" but it ended in tragedy—and with Crane's secret out. The night before New Year's Eve he collapsed, not drunk but hemorrhaging massively from the lungs. Then he had to learn that London gossip was as vicious as New York's— there had been an "orgy" at "Brede."

He struggled to write on and let Cora put the screws on Pinker. But essentially it was the end. He kept Cora well enough deceived so that she set off on a little trip to Paris two hours before he hemorrhaged twice again on March 31. Only after that did she get seriously alarmed and start thinking of drastic measures. And of course it was too late. With infinite trouble to match his patience, she got him to Badenweiler in the Black Forest where on June 5, 1900, not yet twenty-nine, he died. In the mind and writings of no few observers the ghost of Chatterton walked again.

CHAPTER *3*

"His Quality of
Personal Honesty"

HE SENTIMENTALITY, the artistic self-pity and gush
which characterized that Chattertonian tradition and so
much of the writing about Crane after his death, would have
appealed to him not at all. He meant his vision to be as sharp,
clear, and hard as could be, and he meant to be absolutely faithful to it. In the long run the importance of his art depends on the
qualities of that vision and on his great success in compelling his
reader to see life as he saw. Implicit in that vision are ideas which
Crane never began to make intellectually explicit. For that
reason they are as difficult to discuss intelligibly as the ideas
of Henry James. Few commentators have made much effort
to discuss them, and perhaps only one with much success: Daniel
Hoffman in *The Poetry of Stephen Crane*. Obviously, however,
it is essential to every understanding of an artist and his art
that such informing commitments be explained as well as can be.

But once again an examiner runs into a thick fog of ignorance
about Crane's life, in this case the life of his mind. What did
Crane ever read? More important, what did he read before he
wrote the major works? The darkness is lightened almost solely
by Beers's records of hearsay recollected after twenty-five years
or so and by scholarly conjecture. Even when Crane has mentioned (or is said to have mentioned) a book, it is generally
hard to know whether he had read it. Tolstoi was his favorite
author, he testified: was that because he was Howells' favorite?
War and Peace went on and on like Texas, he is supposed to
have remarked: had he read it through? Zola's *Nana* is "honest"
and "Zola is a sincere writer but—is he much good?" Beer quotes
Crane long after he wrote *Maggie*: had he read *Nana* even
then—or heard that he should and glanced at it?

STEPHEN CRANE

Dr. Lars Åhnebrink, in his careful study of Crane in *The Beginnings of Naturalism in American Literature,* shows by many sensitively chosen parallels that Crane might have learned much from a number of Continental authors. But that sort of inference from British readers made Crane explode—though their remarks at literary teas were probably much more *avant garde*-ishly complimentary in intent than he realized. Such questions drove him toward anti-intellectual postures: had he read Mallarmé? Well, no, he didn't know much about "Irish" authors.

I

Perhaps one good way out of the fog is to rise above it and try to see Crane in the aerial perspective of relationships to the movements in thought and attitude of his time, to see him in configuration with the history of ideas. The most prominent feature on the intellectual landscape of the age was disillusion. Then occurred that crisis of idealism, the failure to recover from which marks the end of an era as well as a century and the beginning of "modernity." From the peaks of Jacksonian, trans-cedentalist, evangelical, humanitarian, romantic, and Utopian optimism following the era of good-feeling, Americans had been dropped with a jolt to the disconcerting realities of the Mexican War, the European disasters of 1848, and the moral squalor of the Compromise of 1850. Then came fifteen years of political failure and tragic civil war. Then disastrous cultural revolution in the industrialization and urbanization of culture while the West was raped and the very population altered by the mysteries of massive immigration. In the midst of all this came the shattering ideas as much symbolically as necessarily associated with the names of Darwin and Marx.

The result is the oft-told story of the "Victorian Dilemma." It is a tale of deflation, the reduction of idealism. " 'Twas disillusion upon disillusion," said Robert Frost in "The White-Tailed Hornet." "We were lost piecemeal to the animals, / Like people thrown out to delay the wolves." And among intellectual Americans this process hit its nadir in Crane's time (and largely among those who were his contemporaries like Frederic, Norris, Dreiser, Gertrude Stein, Edwin Arlington Robinson, Masters, and Frost). Most of the others lived to come to some sort of terms with that process which would strike perhaps its deepest notes in *The Mysterious Stranger* and *The Education of Henry Adams*. Crane could not.

It is relevant to Crane's personal case to notice that, in a way, the crisis had been caused by a failure in spiritual resources. Since the Renaissance a steadily increasing intellectual community had been living off the spiritual capital of Christendom. Many efforts to revive, reform, or find a vital substitute for it had failed, and so, finally, had the heritage. In his own way Crane was to recapitulate that process.

Immediately, of course, the crisis for most Americans was a religious one. Crane seems not to have been at all aware of the Marxian considerations which friends as close as Garland and Howells had entertained and rejected. The vital crisis sprang from the threat of Darwinism to reduce man to complete, mere animality and to find the key to his condition in a Machiavellian ethic of pure power. God seemed excluded from the universe; so did spirituality and meaning from the life of man. The ultimate reduction of all thought to a pure, hard naturalism impended. No metaphysics would there approach reality. Cosmology, teleology, and anthropology would fall to the aimless collisions of chance with matter until the triumph of entropy in designless stasis.

No American writer ever wholly accepted that ultimate, though Robinson Jeffers the poet of "inhumanism" perhaps comes closest. Confronted by that prospect, virtually every thinker has wished to reconstitute idealism as well as he could or dared, from the minima of E. A. Robinson's "Credo," Dreiser's triumphant confusion, or Woodbridge's "natural teleology" up through infinite varieties of compromise to various forms of complete neo-ideality. Historically, in the decades prior to Crane there had tended to be a response according to generations. One tended to fly to quick rationalizations if, like Whitman or Lowell, he'd come to maturity amid the ancient comforts. It took a Melville—and a Melville's price—to hold out.

If, however, one had spent his youth secure but found his young maturity threatened by the new thought, the case was interestingly altered. He tended to postpone decision, to take time to let things settle, and to make only minimal decisions meanwhile. He became, perhaps for decades, perhaps for life, an agnostic. That was generally true for the generation more or less thirty in 1870—Twain, Howells, and the James brothers, Peirce, Wright, young Holmes, and the Adams brothers. But what of Crane's group, a generation born into the newness and presented with compromise against which to revolt? The evidence is clear that it was sorely tempted to pay the price, no matter what, and go the whole way. Some eventually announced, impermanently or imperfectly, that they had gone and become total naturalists. In the works of all, the struggle toward or against it is recorded. And, though it does not categorically make him a "naturalist," this is true of Stephen Crane also.

All these tendencies, with special variations for every individual, were operative in the world of family, churches, schools, colleges, books and journalism—in the whole climate of thought and feeling in which Crane grew up. Heuristically it may be helpful to see the ideas and literary attitudes of the time in an interlocking figure of these themes short of naturalism.

The simplest way to take the new thought was to be anti-intellectual—to reject it entirely. Religiously this led to the Fundamentalism which William Jennings Bryan exposed at the Scopes trial. That rejection characteristically went hand in hand with an emotional refusal to see that rural mores did not fit urban-industrial circumstances. And, in spite of itself, Fundamentalism was keyed to the low-brow features of popular culture—in literature especially to the ancient clichés of romantic sentimentality and heroicism which Howells had mocked in his famous simile of the grasshopper. That was the sort of religion and, one suspects, the sort of culture Crane inherited through his mother from the Pecks.

Far more respectable intellectually was the neo-idealism of a Whitman or the "Personalist" philosophers of Syracuse University; or of Sidney Lanier, or Lowell; of Minot J. Savage or John Fiske; of William Graham Sumner or Lester Ward. It might go all the way to Transcendentalism or beyond with Whitman, to a neo-idealistic Christianity with Lanier, Savage, or Fiske. It might erect a mystique of individualism with the "hard" Social Darwinism of Sumner or a mystique of group solidarity with Ward. Howells as Tolstoian was strongly tempted Ward's way. And neo-idealism keyed reality to neo-romanticism in the arts because they were characteristically parallel reactionary modes of thought and feeling. Neo-romanticism was admittedly not a true continuation of Wordsworth and Coleridge, Scott, Shelley, and Keats. Forced to the wall, its adherents confessed that they no longer believed as the Romantics had. They just wanted arts, particularly a literature, into which they could escape from the real world. They wished to forget care, doubt, worry, confusion, and pain and live imaginatively in free sentiment, the exotic, sublime, chivalric, magical, and strenuous. Rider Haggard and then Stevenson and Du Maurier were their men—and the George Eliot of *Romola* their woman. They characteristically held political, social, economic views to match.

The agnostics, on the other hand, suffered the curious advantages of their lack of comfort, their need for courage. Deprived of abstraction and generalization, they had to descend to the concrete particular. Deprived of the divine and spiritual, they descended to the human (and bore resolutely there, refusing to be depressed to the animal). Deprived of the ideal, the sublime, the heroic, they had left the average, the commonplace, the ordinary—for better or worse, they were wed to the common. It was this allegiance which made realism attractive, natural, perhaps almost inevitable for them. It also made their sympathies characteristically democratic, humane, and contemporaneous—and so revisionist, or reformist, perhaps in some way socialistic. In pattern, ignoring all variation and aberrations such as those of Henry and Brooks Adams—one can say that *realist* implied democrat, humanitarian, sceptic, reformer, and anti-imperialist. *Neo-romantic* implied aristocrat, racist, "hard" Darwinist, conservative, and imperialist. And amid all these congeries within American life, immensely more fluid than any scheme could show, Stephen Crane was fated to be a Seeker after the secret of his own vision.

II

Nobody was wholly, purely any of those "types." Everybody was a mixture—and himself. What was Stephen Crane? Again, for lack of evidence there is much one shall never know. And, because of Crane's perpetual youth, there has to be less to know than in a case of achieved maturity. Yet there are interesting and helpful leads toward understanding the intellectual qualities of that vision which was central to Crane and his art.

The first and most essential themes of his thought are religious. For life-reasons, his religion was necessarily rebellious. That did not, however, prevent it from being serious. On the contrary, he absolutely refused to have the blasphemy bowdlerized from *The Black Riders* even though it was to be his first regularly published book; the publisher could keep it in or return the manuscript. As Hoffman intelligently and originally shows, it was the frontier, Calvinistic, minatory evangelicism of the Pecks against which Stephen revolted most violently. The behaviorism of his father's moral tracts and his father's commitment to the church as institution Stephen also rejected—but not his father's gentle intuition of God's love pervading, hidden behind His objective universe, supporting all, quick and tender in mercy.

Proceeding with the inevitable pain of confusion added to the wrath of revolt, Crane groped his way toward a religion of his own. The point which has eluded perhaps most commentators is that he was most *revolté*, most exasperating, most agonized—and probably most creative—when he insisted on taking the heart of the family code seriously. If, instead of practicing bourgeois, institutional respectability, one practiced the virtues of St. Francis and Sir Philip Sidney in Port Jervis or Asbury Park, what then? If one didn't practice those directly, why pretend? Why are non-respectable sins which unite one with common humanity not better than respectable sins which degrade and divide the brotherhood of man? That, one must think, is pretty surely the logic of Stephen Crane in tutelage to mother, family, schools.

He never adolescently denied the reality of sin—his sin. He took obvious pride in confessing himself a bad boy, the family black sheep. His chosen position, however, committed him to one of the permanent themes of his thought. It was that, fully recognizing the slippery multivalences of truth, one must be as absolutely honest as he could. An early reviewer put his finger on an essentially Cranean quality when he spoke of *Maggie's* "daring and terrible directness which in its iconoclasm is the very characteristic of rugged undisciplined strength in a youth of genius."[1] Crane meant to smash icons. But there was that blend his Claverack drill-mate noted in him of "self-depreciation coupled with arrogance" and stimulated by his "fear of ridicule, especially of his own."[2]

Emerson spoke to Crane as to so many of his targets—"the young men of America." From the wall of the old Art Students' League Building which his poverty inhabited, for instance, Crane copied off the Emersonian motto: "Congratulate yourself if you have done something strange and extravagant and broken the monotony of a decorous age."[3] But there was always his need for a saving balance. And so he defined himself in famous words to John Northern Hilliard:

> . . . I understand that a man is born into the world with his own pair of eyes, and he is not at all responsible for his vision— he is merely responsible for his quality of personal honesty. To keep close to this honesty is my supreme ambition. There is sublime egotism in talking of honesty. I, however, do not say that I am honest. I merely say that I am as nearly honest as a weak mental machinery will allow. This aim in life struck me as being the only thing worth while. A man is sure to fail at it, but there is something in the failure.[4]

That arrogance of a self-depreciating iconoclasm also informed Crane's treatment of the tradition from his father which he readapted for his most enduring and fundamental ideal: the Christian gentleman. Since there had been Americans, sensitive men had worked to reconcile that major ideal to American conditions.[5] There are plenty of data to show that Stephen Crane joined their ranks after his fashion. The plainest evidence appears in his confessional letters to Miss Nellie Crouse of Akron, Ohio, written just as *The Red Badge of Courage* made him an international celebrity.

In capsule, when the Aristotelian pattern of the hero was reconciled with the Christian picture of the saint, the resulting chivalric ideal became a beautiful vision reserved for the nobility. In Renaissance times Castiglione's notions of the intellectual and esthetic cultivation of the courtier met in England with the rising power of the landed gentry and the Protestant theory of individual responsibility to convert chivalry into the ideal of the English gentleman. A series of fine compromises secured the values which made England great. Not blood alone (for the class was relatively fluid) but virtue, not wealth alone but cultivation, not manners alone but service to others characterized the complete gentleman. Love and, above all, service to Cross and Crown, to land and house, to tenant as to family: distinguished, objective, unselfish service was the *beau idéal* of the English Gent.

Amid the fluidities and erosions of colonial American life, that ideal was of utmost social importance. To save its essence for the waxing democracy of post-Revolutionary America had been of central intellectual concern to minds as diverse as those of Jefferson, Fenimore Cooper, and Emerson. Demonstrably the ideal had lived among descendants of Jasper and Stephen Crane quite conscious of debts to family and tradition. By 1896 the then current Stephen was trying to prove to a chic and pretty girl that he was not in the popular sense a Bohemian and that a true view of things exposed the foolish exhaustion of both the Bohemian and the conventional views.

In no very logical sequence, Crane let Miss Nellie Crouse see the whole pattern of his ideal. Emptiness and mere conceit make up too nearly all the core of what Society values. Therefore, he dislikes the "society man" and especially the "society matron," with the peculiar iron-like quality of their thick-headedness and the wild exuberance of their vanity. Together they create "the social crisis" (apparently the demand to flaunt one's vanity) which makes Crane "gibber" and fail humiliatingly. The society man is too often an "awful chump" or a "duffer" because his courage, courtesy, and integrity are all for show: "There is an enormous majority who, upon being insured of safety from detection—become at once the most unconventional of peoples." As for "the hordes who hang upon the outskirts of good society and chant 143 masses per day to the social gods and think that because they have money they are well-bred—for such people I have a scorn which is very deep and very intense."

Crane's instinct for his subject was amazingly traditional and precise. "Form really is truth, simplicity," he told Miss Crouse about manners. Again, "I swear by the real aristocrat. The man whose forefathers were men of courage, sympathy, and wisdom, is usually one who will stand the strain whatever it may be. He is like a thoroughbred horse. His manes may be high and he will do a lot of jumping often but in the crisis he settles down

and becomes the most reliable and enduring of created things."
And that he thought such fortitude would ever be called upon
he repeatedly made clear in this odd epistolary courtship.

Mankind he thought doomed to vanity "and the inherent in-
dolence and cowardice which is the lot of all. . . ." Not even
"high aims and things" could save. Most idealists "strike me as
about the worst and most penetrating kind of a bore I know."
They really mean vanity, ". . . and there is a ridiculous quality
to me in all high ambitions, of men who mean to try to make
themselves great because they think it would [be] so nice to be
great, to be admired, to be stared at by the mob." Finally, even
the very few who are sincere are doomed:

> Tolstoy's aim is, I suppose—I believe—to make himself good.
> It is an incomparably quixotic task for any man to undertake.
> He will not succeed; but he will even succeed more than he
> can ever himself know, and so at his nearest point to success he
> will be proportionately blind. This is the pay of this kind of
> greatness.

Was this mere blackness, mere defeatism? Crane had already
tried to assure Nellie Crouse that it was not. He admitted to being "minded to die in my thirty-fifth year." That was all he could
stand. "I don't like to make wise remarks on the aspect of life
but I will say that it doesn't strike me as particularly worth the
trouble. The final wall of the wise man's thought however is
Human Kindness of course. If the road of disappointment, grief,
pessimism, is followed far enough, it will arrive there. Pessimism
itself is only a little, little way, and moreover it is ridiculously
cheap. The cynical mind is an uneducated thing." To be "as kind
and as just as may be" is "the solitary pleasure of life." For
what life offered finally was not pleasure but "a sincere, desperate, lonely battle" against ". . . the majestic forces which
are arrayed against man's true success—not the world—the world
is silly changeable, any of its decisions can be reversed—but
man's own colossal impulses more strong than chains. . . ."

It was of a piece with the tragedy of Crane's life and the
tragicalness of his vision that he failed to enlist Miss Crouse to
fight beside him. The vision, and perhaps Crane's reputation,
frightened her in spite of his assurance that he found the society
girl "charming."[6] It was a frightening vista, taken from a point

of vantage only available to the irony which follows upon bitter disillusion. Little wonder Crane found no girl ready to share it.

The wonder is that there has been so little remark on the intrinsically aristocratic *and* Christian qualities of Crane's vision. One can understand a Crane in a post-Kirkegaardian world more readily than before. Only a man who had seen through to the conceit and hypocrisy behind "the world" and then turned his disillusion ironically upon his own conceit as the critic of other men's sin could have reached Crane's viewpoint. Taken seriously, as an earnest, gifted, and isolated preacher's orphan might take them, the ideals of the Christian gentleman easily exposed the follies of the world. All the rest might come from the mere turning of his honesty back upon himself.

Despite Hoffman's pioneering and some very interesting articles[7] (excluding some fashionable but non-serious efforts at mythical interpretation), Crane's relations with Christianity remain to be definitively studied. The preacher's kid of course commanded a full stock of biblical and churchly allusion, rhythm, and imagery. At the same time, the rebel was most likely of all to be aware when and why he employed them. He could revolt, that is, but not escape. He had nothing but contempt for the charity-working "Christianity as seen around town."[8] But that was because it was "seen"—and because he thought it not Christian. To his own compassion there was no conscious limit: "One of Stephen Crane's characteristics was a haunting solicitude for the comfort and welfare of other people," recalled Frank Noxon, "especially those of narrow opportunity. He thought about it as one thinks about an art or craft, developing a style and inventing original methods."[9] Obviously this compassion was a controlling feature of his literary imagination as well.

That solicitude and perhaps, as Van Wyck Brooks suggests,[10] some deep psychological need of his generation to know squalor and chaos, sent Crane to study the Bowery. But other impulses came also from his relation to gentility. That *méfiance* which prompted Crane to talk Bowery dialect to a sweet young socialite and to treat a midnight streetwalker like a duchess for the benefit of an unwanted literary admirer, also a minister's son,[11] had deep roots. Partly it was disgust at social hypocrisy. But partly also it was Crane's response to feeling *déclassé*. To repeat, as a type the American *déclassé* author has never been studied. Yet his ranks are full and fascinating. They include, among others, Freneau, Cooper, Poe, Emerson, Hawthorne, Melville, Twain, Frank Norris, and Scott Fitzgerald beside Crane. How much of Ishmael's "hypo" did Crane take down to the Bowery? And was Crane the first American in whom the *déclassé* became also the *déraciné*?

III

Those and perhaps less scrutable temperamental or psychic factors lay behind his sense that the essence of life is war. No one has apparently ever challenged the observation that this was Crane's basic sense of life. The evidence is overwhelming. And, if there be no clear explanation of the origin of his idea, he succeeds so well in finding war in every relation of man to man, to woman, to nature, and to institutions that he leaves his reader convinced. The only way to avoid Crane's conviction is to step out of his world into one more tender-minded. War, says Vernall, Crane's *alter ego* in "War Memories": ". . . it is simply life . . ." *Maggie* begins with a skirmish—the slum kids are playing "King of the Hill" with vicious fervor. From first to last in Crane's serious expression, esthetic or not, the vision of war is at the center. One could document it almost endlessly and at random. It lies at the heart of every significant fiction. It is the *donnée* of Crane's imagination.

If one simply accepts that "given" and adds the obvious features of his boyhood, it is easy to see how young Stephen became fascinated by the phenomena of fear and courage. The frail kid who would catch barehanded any ball anybody could pitch in Asbury Park; who pegged down to second base no matter if the pain doubled him up at Syracuse; and who coached, and played quarterback for a flying-wedge, help-the-runner town football team, needed no "actual" war to teach him fear and courage. He would find his knowledge confirmed at the wars.

Crane knew about the physical phenomena of fear in many guises—the panic of *The Red Badge,* the "eels of despair [which] lay wet and cold against [the] back" of the New York Kid in "The Five White Mice"[12]—but he was mainly inclined to define and dramatize fear as anything the coward permitted to interfere with courage. And he achieved an exact and admirably useful definition of courage which interestingly anticipates that of Ernest Hemingway.

This definition properly occurs most overtly in non-fictional pieces. He loved locomotive engineers, for instance. A Greek who, wounded, persisted in driving one through barrages Crane called "a daisy." But, reporting for McClure on "The Scotch Express," he said it just right:

> It should be a well-known fact that, all over the world, the engine-driver is the finest type of man that is grown. He is the pick of the earth. He is altogether more worthy than the soldier, and better than the men who move on the sea in ships. He is not paid too much; nor do his glories weight his brow; but for outright performance, carried on constantly, coolly, and without elation, by a temperate, honest, clear-minded man, he is the further point. And so the lone human at his station in a cab, guarding money, lives, and the honor of the road, is a beautiful sight. The whole thing is aesthetic.[13]

To put it that way, finding the highest and best—and the beautiful—in the daily commonplace was the essence of literary realism. But Crane did not always put it so. His revised account of the action in which he himself finally achieved patent heroism —the Marine raid at Guantanamo—is worth quoting from at length. It contains other notes:

> Then the bullets began to snap, snap, snap, at his head, while all the woods began to crackle like burning straw. I could lie near and watch the face of the signalman, illumed as it was by the yellow shine of lantern-light, and the absence of excitement, fright, or any emotion at all on his countenance was something to astonish all theories out of one's mind. The face was in every instance merely that of a man intent upon his business, the business of wig-wagging into the gulf of night where a light on the *Marblehead* was seen to move slowly.
>
> These times on the hill resembled, in some ways, those terrible scenes on the stage—scenes of intense gloom, blinding lightning, with a cloaked devil or assassin or other appropriate character muttering deeply amid the awful roll of the thunder-drums. It was theatric beyond words: one felt like a leaf in this booming chaos, this prolonged tragedy of the night. Amid it all one could see from time to time the yellow light on the face of a preoccupied signalman. . . .

Clancy had to return to the top of the ridge and outline himself and his flag against the sky . . . as soon as the Spaniards caught sight of this silhouette, they let go like mad at it. To make things more comfortable for Clancy, the situation demanded that he face the sea and turn his back to the Spanish bullets. This was a hard game, mark you—to stand with the small of your back to volley firing. Clancy thought so. Everybody thought so. We all cleared out of his neighborhood. . . .

I watched his face, and it was as grave and serene as that of a man writing in his own library. He was the very embodiment of tranquility in occupation. He stood there amid the animal-like babble of the Cubans, the crack of rifles, and the whistling snarl of the bullets, and wigwagged . . . without heeding anything but his business. There was not a single trace of nervousness or haste. . . .

To say the least, a fight at close range is absorbing as a spectacle. No man wants to take his eyes from it until that time comes when he makes up his mind to run away. To deliberately stand up and turn your back to a battle is in itself hard work. To deliberately stand up and turn your back to a battle and hear immediate evidences of the boundless enthusiasm with which a large company of the enemy shoot at you from an adjacent thicket is, to my mind at least, a very great feat.[14]

There are true ambivalences of treatment and appeal in this account between dry, rather deprecating, and lush, heroic tones. They evidence a real ambivalence in the author. He was torn between loyalties both natural and preferential to the emotions and modes of the realists and those of the Rooseveltian, "strenuous life" neo-romanticists.

IV

On or about December 1, 1895, William Dean Howells received one of the most extraordinary fan letters in a long literary life not devoid of surprise. He had favorably reviewed in his *Harper's Weekly* column a book called *Red Men and White* written by a younger friend to whom he had given literary advice nearly ten years before. The letter read:

I have just got through with reading your "Life and Letters" on Wister—For one who protests so much ignorance you come more nearly telling just what Wister is doing (*"TRUTH"*—) than any other fellow who is set in judgment on things of the sort. Wister is a great man and it gives me comfort to know that he will help me by his success to make people see *"the thing"* which is my soul. When one thinks that when I drew 'scouts— soldiers—injuns'—it was the worst of form to treat such 'red eyed' red covered—unreal stuff—it gives me courage to have you think Wister will finally bring home to such as you—*the thing*—the truth—however much you may not care for it. I wish that this had happened before Thanksgiving.

Frederic Remington[15]

With full allowance for temperament, Remington's anger half veiled in praise reflected resentments held by a group of Americans to whom Howells had indeed given scant consideration. They embodied the spirit of a gambling culture. They were lovers of action and competition——of pitting oneself against nature, against pain and pressure, against other men. They were sportsmen. As climbers, hunters, and fishermen they loved wildness. As boxers and wrestlers, rowers and runners, inventive developers of baseball, football, basketball, and hockey, they were changing the face and tone of American life, most especially in the colleges. Their popular following grew phenomenally. Sports expressed the essence of American culture perhaps more directly than anything else. And they were beginning to achieve a literature published representatively in the magazines of the House of Harpers from which Howells was parting just as Stephen Crane came seriously on the scene. Henry Mills Alden, in defiance both of his friend Howells and of his own literary convictions, was printing the fiction of Wister, the non-fiction of Roosevelt, and the pictures of Remington.

That was not a literature, as it was not a quality of life, attractive to the Dean of American Letters. He was prepared to agree that sports were healthful and emotionally appropriate for the young. But he hoped they would grow up and sober down. He hoped Americans would grow away from frontier bully-boy muscularity toward civilization, would leave gambling for creativity, passion for discipline, competition for cooperation. To him the most shocking fact about American life was precisely that it *was* a shrieking World of Chance, brutalized, corrupted, and too often blood-spattered by dog-eat-dog ethics. His long war with the neo-romantics was being fought on one side over just that issue. His delight in "banging the Babes of Romance about" rose from his derision of the ridiculous sentimentalities, the flossy pomposities and foolish sublimities of century-old clichés. But ethically he was determined to raise his public to the highest level of sensitive and responsible civilization. At best the sportsmen and their writers looked atavistic to Howells. At worst they looked as Theodore Roosevelt hunting bears for sport looked to the memorialist of *Mark Twain in Eruption*.

How things looked to Howells, of course, made a great difference to Stephen Crane. Crane felt "indelibly indebted" not only for friendship but for literary guidance and enlightenment. He had rejoiced to enlist in "the beautiful war" for realism, and he gave thanks that experience proved him allied neither "to the Chump in Art or even to the Semi-Chump in Art."[16] The fact that Crane dared use such sporty language with the Dean evidenced two important aspects of their relationship, however. Both understood that Crane was to be no little Howells, but wholly Stephen Crane. And among his many intellectual tensions was that between the pole of Howells' complex, mature vision of a responsible and humane life and art and the pole of the Remington-Wister-TR doctrine.

The most contagious form of neo-romanticism, the Rooseveltian attitude was the one least vulnerable to the ironies of Howells, Twain, and Veblen. It probably played a decisive role in the defeat of the realists in their fight for American taste in the 1890's. More significantly, its mood was to sweep the nation into the Spanish-American and Philippine wars, into imperialism, international adventure, and eventual major power status. A muscular, buoyant, college-bred elite, represented primarily but by no means uniquely in TR, had sprung from the Gilded Age. After many terms in the presidency since Jackson, observed Howells upon Roosevelt's ascension to the White House, the "simple men" had been fated by conditions in the republic to give way again to the "gentle men" [he carefully separated the words]. In the '90's that elite was wooing the psyche of the nation preparatory to taking over power. The inherent conflict between realism and all it implied and muscular neo-romanticism was what Remington, Yale football player, bankrupt stockman, and avowed "romantic"[17] was finally getting at.

The attractions of "the strenuous life" for Crane were many, but compromised. His sense of war and cult of courage had much to do with it. The perplexities of Silas Lapham or Basil March might be real enough, even agonizing, in the moral context of civilization. But other impulses, admittedly uncivilized, stirred Crane's imagination. Striving to make copy of nothing much on the way to Greece, he wrote an odd, revealing bit into an account of the movements of a British battleship's boat:

> Down in the launch . . . there was a middy who was a joy. He was smaller than a sparrow, but—my soul—how bright and Napoleonic and forcible he was! . . . She would be a fool of a Mother who would trust him in a pantry where there were tarts, and his big sister can box his ears for some years to come, but of course there is no more fiery-hearted scoundrel in the fleet of the Powers than this babe. Of course he would drop to his knees and pray his Admiral a hundred prayers if by this he could be at his station on the *Camperdown*, and have her move into action immediately. Against what? Against anything. This is of the traditions that perforce are in the breast of the child. . . . If another child of the *Camperdown* should steal this child's knife he might go to a corner and perhaps almost shed tears, but no hoary admiral can dream of the wild slaughter and Hades on the bosom of the sea that agitate this babe's breast. He is a damned villain. And yet may the God of Battle that sits above the smoke watch over this damned villain and all bright, bold, little damned villains like him![18]

Something of the same neo-romantic *panache* occasionally overcame Crane in Cuba—or when, especially at the end of his life, he wrote in desperate haste for money. Experience, however, always restored the balance his irony demanded. The awful bathos which overcame the braggart, soon-defeated Greeks set Crane to writing amazingly like the Hemingway who was to become in important ways so amazingly like him anyway. He interviewed defeated Greek soldiers, and one much impressed him:

> In the photograph galleries in Athens there are many portraits of bearded gentlemen in kilts festooned with 500 yards of cartridge belt and gripping their Gras rifles ferociously. . . . I know that type too, and I have never seen them do anything. Generally speaking, they are a pack of humpty-dumptys. But this brown-

faced, quiet lad, with his lamb-like eyes and gently considerate
ways, I know him too, and he will stick to a trench, and stick
and stick and go without water and food and fight long and
still stick until the usual orders come to fall back. . . .

The soldier answers his question:

"I am a soldier. I have been fortunate enough to have been
wounded for Greece. I have lived on nothing practically for
months, and marched many miles and fought a few battles. I
have a right to name any man whom I am sure has not done his
duty by Greece, and I name the crown prince."
"Did he not say, or at least was he not reported to have
said at Domokos that there he would stand or fall with his men?"
"Yes, such was the report. But where is Domokos now? In the
hands of the Turks. . . . These quotable sentiments are sometimes
unfortunate. I know from experience."
"Why?"
"Well, when I left Athens there was a considerable celebration
by my family and friends. Tears and flowers, added to a Spartan
injunction from my mother. I believe I replied with a Spartan
sentence too. It is very difficult."[19]

If irony cut down Crane's romanticism, so did compassion.
His "haunting solicitude" for others shattered any capacity for
smugness he might have had. It reached out to the physical
suffering of animals and people. War-wounded and refugees
naturally moved him deeply. Of the Greeks he wrote, "Their
plight makes a man hate himself for being well fed and having
some place to go. . . . There is no food. . . . It is a case for the
opening of skies, but no skies open. I wish I knew what is to
become of these poor people."[20] He found it useful to advise his
readers that, "There is more of this sort of thing in war than
glory and heroic death, flags, banners, shouting, and victory."[21]
And, of course, the same thing went for psychic pain. He described the heartbreak of Cuban wives and children when
Spanish fathers were forcibly repatriated at the end of the war.
It was easy to say: " 'Serves them right; why didn't they take
up with men of their own people, instead of with Spaniards?'
But, after all—and after all—and again after all, it is human
agony and human agony is not pleasure."[22]

V

On the other hand, Crane's vision and temperament were too aristocratic (and perhaps too natively Calvinist) to let him sympathize with the democratic or Tolstoian humanitarianism of a Garland, Howells, or Edward Bellamy. The bitter humor of his suggestion that an American Academy consist wholly of Edwin Markham has been lamentably misread.[23] One of Crane's last journalistic efforts, this was a bit of "paragraphing" sarcastically expressing his contempt of the very idea of American "immortals," in spite of the fact "that we can show more fine old litterateurs with manes of snow-white hair than any country on the face of the globe" and have a noble race of college presidents busily raiding the wealth of Chicago. But he was equally contemptuous of the Whitmanian:

And what then? One's thoughts instinctively turn to Edwin Markham. Mr. Markham is of that virile manhood which expresses itself by appearing in public in its shirt sleeves; a strong man, Mark ye; no apish child of fashion; a veritable eagle of freedom, and, withall, kindly, tender to the little lame lamb—I, bold, yet gentle, defiant of all convention, and yet simple in his manner even to kings. Such a man is Edwin Markham.

Very good. We have made a fair start. We have one leonine old man in his shirt sleeves. We proceed, much encouraged. Who is worthy to take a place by the side of the illustrious coatlessness? Let us make haste. The name of W. D. Howells occurs to somebody. But, no; he wears collars. It is known; it is common talk. He has never had his photograph taken while enwrapped in a carelessly negligent bath towel. In the name of God, let us have virility; let us look for the wild, free son of nature. Mark Twain? At first it seems that he would have a chance. He growls out his words from the very pit of his stomach and is often uncivil to strangers. But, no; he, too, wears collars and a coat.

For a moment we are stunned with a sense of defeat. But, no; an inspiration comes. Why have forty members to an American Academy? Let us have only one. Call Markham; frame him up; give him a constitution and a set of by-laws; let him convene himself and discuss literary matters. Then we have an American Academy.[24]

This was the Crane who observed of another sentimental reformer that Miss Frances Willard's "affair with Miss Willard should be stopped by the police."[25]

Always alienated from the folksy, Gospel of Wealth-worshiping *bourgeoisie*, Crane was typically marooned between the aristocratic neo-romantics and their realist-reformer opponents. The one seemed brutally fatuous, the other sentimental. Mrs. Howells was quite right, he told one inquiring lady, that he had "no opinion of missions." He disliked the whole relationship. Briefly in the bush with Cuban partisans, he had witnessed their incredible capacity to endure hunger, fatigue, and pain. With the army, he saw their equal uselessness as regular soldiers. The Cuban fighting man, he concluded, "exists with the impenetrable indifference or ignorance of the greater part of the people in an ordinary slum. Everybody knows that the kind of sympathetic charity which loves to be thanked is often grievously disappointed and wounded in tenement districts. . . . The Cubans accept our stores in something of this way."[26] And, he implies, that is as it should be in both cases; it is in the nature of things.

Inevitability did not, however, lend glamor to the deprived in Crane's eyes. He could sympathize with the pathos of their condition. Investigating "Opium's Varied Dreams"[27] for his study of New York, he found that it was "the 'sporting' class" of the Tenderloin which most took it up—"cheap actors, race track touts, gamblers, and the different kinds of confidence men. . . ." He found them neither glamorous nor victimized. They saw no gorgeous dreams, he held. But they found "a fine languor, a complete mental rest. . . . Wrong departs, injustice vanishes; there is nothing but a quiet harmony of all things—until the next morning." Of course this "lie" is most eagerly embraced by "the people of the Tenderloin: they who are at once supersensitive and hopeless . . . but they awake to find the formidable labors of life grown more formidable"—and hit the pipe again. In short, "the root of Bowery life," as he told Mrs. Howells' enquiring friend, was "a sort of cowardice."[28] That was what his long investigation of the poor had taught him.

By the same token, he was not in the least impressed with the innate nobility of the common man. The heroism of individual Greek soldiers had utterly shamed their poltroon of a Crown Prince, Crane thought. But he was most negatively affected by the sight of a civilian demagogue's failure to manipulate a disgruntled crowd to turn the disaster to political account. There are buried memories of the post-Periclean contemptibility of the *demos* in Crane's story of how "the man in the white hat" brought his mob to the palace and left it agitating before a single evzone sentry while he went inside. There rose "the audible machinery, the temper of the people, revolving and revolving toward turbulence":

> Once the humming of voices in its crescendo almost reached the point of action. Then this kilted soldier, this simple child of the hills, darted a look at the crowd, and this look was so full of scorn, deep and moving scorn, that it must have been felt to the pits of their stomachs. He stooped and picked from the ground a handful of pebbles. He raised his arm and, still profoundly deliberate and with supreme disdain, this solitary figure on the palace steps flung the handful of pebbles straight into the upturned faces of the Athenians.[29]

Likewise the racism and its correlative imperialism of his age affected Crane ambiguously. From Cuba he wrote that Americans must learn to put more "peacock feathers into our business" because these people "not only admire splendor, they reverence it." "Mediterranean" peoples, he considered, lack "the sense of public navigation." And in Havana "they are children of pellucid chance . . . joyously irresponsible and incompetent."[30] Yet his playlet *The Blood of the Martyr* anticipates in intent (though not skill) the savage anti-imperialism of Mark Twain's 'To the Person Sitting in Darkness."

It was in connection with this question, when the issue was tearing at the roots of the American conscience, and Americans were dividing angrily over whether to play the imperial game or not, that Crane expressed his ideal of intellectual courage as a corollary of his ideal of courage in general. Americans were exercised about the Philippines and Britons about South Africa, and everybody saw the parallels. Crane heartily approved a British protest because there was in it no hint of the "Boston . . . Great Movement . . ." mood, and it would "get no extra British soldiers killed in the Transvaal. . . . There is no screaming. . . . Instead of being the letter of a fiery agitator, it is the letter of a saddened man":

It all plainly resolves itself to a nationalistic basis. One hardly knows how to state it. One has the burning wish for the quick success of the American arms in the Philippines. At the same time, one has a still more burning wish that the Filipinos shall see us as just men, willing, anxious to deal fairly, govern with studious equity; depart, if need be, with honor.

However, Mr. Watson failed to express that comic vanity which leads one to long that the enemy should know that one is an honorable man. It could not possibly be admitted as necessary, but still Mr. Watson does not send any statement to the Boers assuring them that the English are honorable men. The feeling is certain to have been in Mr. Watson's bosom, but he said nothing. In these immense things one may have to watch the revolving of ponderous wheels with respect. A socialist cannot be sure what is best for the world at the moment as a paregoric, as a sleeping powder or as a disinfectant.[31]

What became essential to intelligence, Crane thought, was avoidance of that "comic vanity" in all its forms; yet avoidance was only relatively possible. Man was trapped in fate, nature, society, ignorance, and the partial rules of things. Of symbolic Private Nolan, Crane wrote: "Maybe someday, in a fairer, squarer land, he'll get his picture in the paper, too."[32] But for now he is non-respectable, nobody. On the other hand, "When a man is respectable he is fettered to certain wheels, and when the chariot of fashion moves, he is dragged along at the rear. For his agony, he can console himself with the law that if a certain thing has not yet been respectable, he need only wait a sufficient time and it will eventually be so. The only disadvantage is that he is obliged to wait until other people wish to do it, and he is likely to lose his own craving."[33]

Convention generally was as inherently foolish as Cuban courting customs. Men and women everywhere seek, find, and love. And all the "barbed wire entanglements . . . and all the circumlocution and bulwarks and clever football interference and trouble and delay and protracted agony and duenas count for nothing, count for nothing against the tides of human life, which are in Cuba or Omaha controlled by the same moon."[34]

It had long been conventional for romantic artists to be anti-conventional and put their trust in the tides of that "same moon" in Nature. Vigorous by conviction as by habit, sports-loving

Crane adored the open air and knew his own mystique of nature. It is merely notorious, however, that the belief that "Nature never did betray the heart that loved her" moved Crane to black derision. A sad, even silent, anti-conventionality was a stalwart part of his faith. "The lives of some people are one long apology. Mine was, once, but not now," he informed Nellie Crouse. "I go through the world unexplained, I suppose." And again, "You have no idea how it simplifies matters."[35] But it was no primal sanity of natural simplicity he sought—like Whitman or Thoreau. He did not believe in it and never knew it.

" 'The Sense of a City is War,' " said Crane, naming a picture in Linson's studio.[36] And he expanded the idea in an early sketch portraying how at first the stillness of the gold and green countryside seemed "incredibly monotonous" to vacationing city dwellers, "to the warriors from the metropolis. The sense of a city is battle." At length, however, "the song of the universal religion, the mighty and mystic hum of nature," silenced them with a comprehension of "the sacrilege of speech."[37] This matches the fine lantern-light on the water poem from *War is Kind* where the "chorus of colors" confirms the music of the stars:

> Small glowing pebbles
> Thrown on the dark plane of evening
> Sing good ballads of God. . . .[38]

More often nature is ominous. In Mexico, ". . . no one feels like talking in the presence of these mountains that stand like gods on the world, for fear that they might hear."[39] Frequently Crane sees nature as terrible—as to the Nebraska farmers, or the streets of Fort Romper, or to the drowning sailor. War rages there, too. But, as almost everyone has agreed, and as the correspondent in "The Open Boat" perceives, in Crane nature is "flatly indifferent." And when a man knows that and "the pathos of his situation," he has, given the conditions of all the rest of his situation, only courage left—and irony.

VI

Irony is not an idea but a tactic. It is a way of taking the world slantwise, on the flank. It is probably necessary to suppose that the ironic capacity, in any of its modes, is temperamental. Temper informs the ironist's ideas and edges them. It is lucky if it be not wounded itself by them and goaded to despair. Some ironists keep sanguinely balanced like Franklin, some preserve sanctuaries of hope like Howells, some go down like Twain or Henry Adams. Along with his other gifts, a most striking fact about Crane is his possession of an irony so powerful, so deep, and so his own at an age so young. No serious student of the complex, partially understood phenomenon we call by that name can now afford to neglect the irony of Stephen Crane.

No one should suppose that an artist and critic of life and self so sensitive as Crane was ignorant of how thoroughly irony pervaded both explicitly his logical and implicitly his imaginative expression. In the tale, "His Majestic Lie," of a young American spy who sneaks back to Havana, risking death by torture (as Crane had far more remotely done by infiltrating Havana as a correspondent before the occupation), Crane might almost have been defining himself in the character of the hero:

> Johnnie was a typical American . . . a young man of great energy, ready to accomplish a colossal thing for the basic reason that he was ignorant of its magnitude. In fact he attacked all obstacles in life in a spirit of contempt, seeing them smaller than they were until he had actually surmounted them—when he was likely to be immensely pleased with himself. Somewhere in him there was a sentimental tenderness, but it was like a light seen afar at night; it came, went, appeared again in a new place, flickered, flared, went out, left you in a void and angry. And if his sentimental tenderness was a light, the darkness in which it puzzled you was his irony of soul. This irony was directed first at himself; then at you; then at the nation and the flag; then at God. It was a midnight in which you searched for the little elusive, ashamed spark of tender sentiment. Sometimes you thought this was all pretext, the manner and the way of fear of the wit of others; sometimes you thought he was a hardened savage; usually you did not think, but waited in the cheerful certainly that in time the little flare of light would appear in the gloom.[40]

Applied strictly to Crane, however, the "directions" of the irony would have to be revised somewhat. His ironies (for they were various) were directed first at himself; then at you; then at the nation and the flag—and at all abstract conventions and pomposities; then at God; then at Man; and most finally back at himself again. The ultimate stretch of Crane's irony was its enabling him to revolt against his own revolt—because that, too, was based on vanity.

"Vanity of vanities, all is vanity, saith the Preacher," in that most ironic of all books. The sense of the word there is, of course, its root meaning of "emptiness." But Crane would have applied it in both that and its modern sense of "conceit." He saw it everywhere and derided it. In himself: "When I reached twenty-one years and first really scanned my personal egotism I was fairly dazzled by the size of it," he wrote Nellie Crouse. "The Matterhorn could be no more than a tenpin to it."[41]

And he remarked it in others repeatedly as he investigated life. The poor had it. His story "An Experiment in Misery" had shown that not only "cowardice" but "their present state of conceit" damned Bowery folk. "A person who thinks himself superior to the rest of us because he has no job and no pride and no clean clothes [had that at one point been Stephen Crane?] is as badly conceited as Lillian Russell."[42] But the matching piece, "An Experiment in Luxury," told a still more damning tale of the rich. It was a lie that the very rich were miserable; they lived in a beauty and freedom as well as comfort and security unknown to the squalid. And they were not responsible for the difference: "Nobody is responsible for anything. I wish to Heaven somebody was, and then we could all jump him. . . ." The experimenter is made to feel that "all this had merely happened; the great secret hand had guided them here and had guided others there. The eternal mystery of the social condition exasperated him at this time. He wondered if incomprehensible justice were the sister of open wrong."

But the discovery of this experiment is that princely luxury delivers itself at last into vicious but dreary sins of pride. It all came to center in "The Gold Woman," the society matron, the "dragon," of joyless, "terrible pride," with the face of "a grim old fighter . . . for place before the white altars of social excellence." There "was the true abode of conservatism—in the mothers"—savage chieftainesses—"controlled" by "tradition and superstition" who "respected themselves with a magnitude of respect heaven seldom allows on earth." Yet luxury was pleasant.

If the rich "were fairly virtuous," he concluded, the experimenter "could see no reason why they should be so persistently pitied. And no doubt they would dispense their dollars like little seeds upon the soil of the world if it were not for the fact that since the days of the ancient great political economist, the more exalted forms of virtue have grown to be utterly impracticable."[43]

Like the works of the great realists, Crane's are often studies in vision, in discovery, in revelation. And a critique which studied them as exercises in the uneditorialized revelation of human vanity, its consequences, and its meaning would return major rewards in fresh, deep understanding.

For the ultimate twist of Crane's irony came from his perception that man's ridiculous, wicked conceit was necessary to his existence in nature and society. In "The Blue Hotel," because the idea is not the point of the story (though is necessary to a grasp of the point) and the economy of the short story was pressing him, Crane permitted himself an authorial intrusion. Flushed with hubris, the Swede leaves the hotel, stepping out into the symbolic rage of the blizzard from which he will take refuge in the saloon where he will be murdered. In the midst of the tempest, Crane commented, "One viewed the existence of man as a marvel, and conceded a glamor of wonder to these lice which were caused to cling to a whirling, fire-smitten, ice-locked, disease-stricken, space-lost bulb. The conceit of man was explained by this storm to be the very engine of life. One was a coxcomb not to die in it."

And the same was true of man in society. Crane in 1894 grasped the same sense of the raucous fun of slum-life which Howells had registered in *A Hazard of New Fortunes*. They were forgetting death, Howells suggested. Riding home in the cars from Coney Island with the drunk and rowdy, Crane imagined himself in converse with a "Philosopher" who commented on the scene: "I see revealed more clearly the purposes of the inexorable universe which plans to amuse us occasionally to keep us from the rebellion of suicide. And I see how simply and drolly it accomplishes its end. The insertion of a mild quantity of the egotism of sin into the minds of these young men causes them to wildly enjoy themselves. . . . This return of the people to their battles always has a stupendous effect upon me . . . the gaiety which arises upon these Sunday night occasions . . . [has]

an unspeakable air of recklessness and bravado and grief about it. . . . You can hear the undercurrent of it in that song, which is really as grievous as the cry of a child. If he had no vanity— well, it is fortunate for the world that we are not all great thinkers."[44]

If man's vanity was absurd, it was also necessary—and there- fore tragic. And it ended finally in mystery for Crane. He had nothing at all of that smug confidence about summing up the universe in neat formulae eventually available to every school- boy which characterized the popular scientism—and some of the serious science and philosophy—of the day. On the contrary, much of Crane's most intimate expression, particularly his reli- gious poetry, suggests that, for all the mind of man can tell, God, intentionally or not, is playing games with us. The sug- gestion of King Lear is not out of keeping.

One of the missed opportunities of American intellectual life in the latter nineteenth century, as Herbert W. Schneider pointed out some years ago, was the chance Darwinism afforded theologians to construct a new Calvinism. Edwards had done it after deism; the neo-orthodox would do it after Freud. Perhaps Kierkegaard did it for his age—but he was unknown in this country. Temperamentally and imaginatively—though not of course theologically—Crane expressed that possibility in his art and view. In the end, what one means by his irony is that, while Crane was sometimes a romantic, an adventurous boy, he was also a tough-minded realist with a tragic vision more Calvinistic, in its perceptions of the blasphemy as well as the necessity of man's conceit, than naturalistic. He guessed at an ultimate war with God. And he had a nearly Kierkegaardian sense of the ridiculousness of the situation. He could not finally take himself or man seriously in realistic, tragic, naturalistic, Calvinistic, nor, of course, neo-romantic perspectives.

The last irony was directed even against Crane's own moral fight. Then, as in the most moving of Crane's personal docu- ments, his letters to Nellie Crouse, it made him one with Shake- speare, Melville, and Clemens. "The final wall of the wise man's thought . . . ," he concluded, "is Human Kindness"—and then, with a last self-deprecation, "of course." Christian gentleman *manqué*, he was in as thorough revolt against respectability and moralism as Henry James, Sr., but without that worthy's counter-illumination. He groped for an absolute vision. He would have settled for a piety and morality of pity, sympathy, of open humanity. But he was not sure. At twenty-eight Crane died in the heroic but painful condition of soul Keats diagnosed in Shakespeare as "negative capability."

Crane's Art before
The Red Badge of Courage

THE MODERN ERA of appreciation and analysis of the art of Stephen Crane was launched in 1950 by the roughly simultaneous publications of John Berryman's biography and of William M. Gibson's *Stephen Crane: Selected Prose and Poetry*. Two critics more opposite in temperament it would be hard to find. Yet, working independently, Gibson's sensitivity to Crane's best work ratified, in large, Berryman's. For irrelevant reasons not including *The Red Badge* until a second edition, Gibson selected *Maggie*, "The Open Boat" paired with its journalistic predecessor "Stephen Crane's Own Story," "The Bride Comes to Yellow Sky," "The Monster," "The Blue Hotel," a meager sprinkling of poems but including "A Man adrift on a slim spar," and the significant interview with Howells, "Fears Realists Must Wait."

This collection was followed by Robert W. Stallman's exciting first effort to gather "the best" of Crane's work in *Stephen Crane: an Omnibus* (1952). Stallman reprinted virtually all of Gibson plus part of "On the New Jersey Coast," and "The Men in the Storm," "An Experiment in Misery," *George's Mother*, *The Red Badge of Courage*, "A Mystery of Heroism," "The Upturned Face," "An Episode of War," "Stephen Crane's Vivid Story of the Battle of San Juan," a swatch of *Commodore* press stories not by Crane, "The Knife," "His New Mittens," and a group of letters. For some odd reason he omitted "The Monster." When Gibson returned in 1956 with a second edition, he added "The Men in the Storm," "Five White Mice," "Regulars Get No Glory," "The Price of the Harness," and "An Episode of War," as well as *The Red Badge* to it.

Crane's Art *before* The Red Badge of Courage

The point of this listing is that we have been witnessing the establishment of a Crane canon by consensus for over a decade. It is most uncertain and unsatisfactory with regard to the poetry, and it is regrettable that Hoffman has had no chance to edit his selection. Richard Chase in 1960, for instance, selected *Maggie, George's Mother, The Red Badge,* "The Veteran," "A Mystery of Heroism," "An Episode of War," "The Blue Hotel," "The Bride Comes to Yellow Sky," "The Open Boat," "Stephen Crane's Own Story," "The Monster," and some poems for his edition. The consumers for whom these volumes have been prepared are for the most part college students.

Yet, if the canon has been academically, even pedagogically determined, criticism has more reflected than affected its determination. In 1952 Stallman deliberately challenged American critics to produce a body of Crane analysis adequate to Crane's art. Almost without exception, the response has confirmed the canon basically selected by Berryman, Gibson, and Stallman. Regarding them in general, one is led to wonder how much representative critics have read of Crane beyond the textbooks.

While academically sufficient, it should be added, that canon is not critically adequate. A real difficulty is the unavailability of Crane's writing. The Knopf *Work of Stephen Crane* is rare, very expensive when it can be found, and disintegrating from use in many libraries. It necessarily lacked important parts of what Crane wrote. More modern editions show justifiable anxiety over their unavoidable compromises with the problem of establishing the texts. In short, as with most other major American authors, Crane badly needs a complete, definitive edition prepared as reliably as modern bibliographical science will permit. He will get it when the necessary funds become available. In the meanwhile—and in addition—we need a "giant" or a two-volume "Best of Stephen Crane," also reliably edited, for the general reader. He deserves to know a Crane beyond the scope of the present canon.

Not that the present canon is a bad, an outworn or exhausted thing. It goes far toward defining the probably permanent Crane and in establishing his major credentials as an artist. One sound way to survey his reputation and examine the state of Crane criticism would be to take up the major items in that canon in a rough order of their genesis together with their criticism.

Some of the inescapable issues, however, are too large to attach to any single work. Therefore, this study takes up Crane's art and the critical tradition in three natural groupings. One chapter must concern *The Red Badge of Courage*. It is preceded by this one treating of the work before and followed by a third treating of the work after that masterpiece.

I

William Dean Howells always refused to consider that *The Red Badge* was Crane's masterpiece. He liked *Maggie, George's Mother*, the Bowery tales and midnight sketches better. He liked the tough-minded, clear-sighted, disillusioned investigator who saw through conventions and sentimentalities to the facts of social war and was solicitous of its victims. He hoped Crane would outgrow his literary playing with soldiers and his black-rider wars with heaven. Howells sensed, perhaps had even been told about, the early conversion of Crane's literary ideal from a Kipling-like[1] neo-romanticism to Howells' realism. He may—and should—have sensed the tentativeness of that conversion. There remained Crane's constant temptations toward neo-romanticism, at least of a Rooseveltian stripe. And there was that "secret" which Howells saw existed but never guessed at in Crane, the unfathomable something which held him convinced that war everywhere—with God, nature, men, and self—was the irreducible, tragic condition of man.

In short, the Crane who learned what he had to know before he could write *The Red Badge* was multivalent. He had an ideal of realism which had supplanted but not suppressed a boyish ideal of romance. And he had at last immitigably a self which could not be contained in either camp, which has always successfully eluded categorization, and which broke out in unpremeditated, startling verse at the first peak of his creative powers.

It is that multivalence which accounts for his ability to produce the several *Sullivan County Sketches* at the same time as he was struggling toward the first printed *Maggie* and the half-realized "Midnight Sketches." In the admirable introduction to Melvin Schoberlin's edition of *The Sullivan County Sketches* (1949)—which was to have accompanied his lamentably never-published definitive life of Crane—the key to the situation first appeared. Writing to Lily Brandon Munroe, Crane confided that he had "renounced the clever school in literature" and "my clever Rudyard Kipling style" for a creed

> . . . identical with the one of Howells and Garland and in this way I became involved in the beautiful war between those who say that art is man's substitute for nature and we are the most successful in art when we approach the nearest to nature and truth, and those who say—well, I don't know what they say. Than that they can't say much but they fight villainously and keep Garland and I out of the big magazines. . . . The two years of fighting have been well-spent. . . . They used to call me "that terrible, young radical," but now they are beginning to hem and haw and smile—those very old coons who used to adopt a condescending air toward me. There is an irony in the present situation that I enjoy, devil take them for a parcel of old, cringing, conventionalized hens.[2]

There had been little to flutter the "hens" about the Sullivan sketches, however, except perhaps a youthful exuberance in the author. If there were, as Schoberlin justly says, signs of Stephen Crane emerging from the chrysalis, the sketches belonged to an ancient tradition of American sporting, out-of-doors, masculine humor—what is often loosely called "frontier" humor with its established techniques of slapstick, burlesque, and "the sell." Before Crane's running afoul of the sloppy parade of the Junior Order of American Mechanics in his Asbury Park correspondence and his embarrassing Whitelaw Reid politically, the *New York Tribune* had printed five sketches, one each Sunday, in July, 1892. After that *The Cosmopolitan*, in reaction against Howells who had explosively ceased to be its editor on June 30, bought one.

Less filled with "clever and witty expedients" than Crane supposed, his sketches contained true foreshadowings of greatness. Perhaps the most wholly successful is the one wholly without slapstick: "Killing His Bear, a Winter Tragedy with Three Actors"—the bear, a hound, and "the little man." In the frozen woods the man waits. "On the ridge-top a dismal choir of hemlocks crooned over one that had fallen. The dying sun created a dim purple and flame-colored tumult on the horizon's edge. . . . A gray, ponderous stillness came heavily in the steps of the sun." And on the stillness breaks the belling of the dog: "a hound, as he nears large game, has the griefs of the world on his shoulders, and his baying tells of the approach of death. He is sorry he came." When the man "saw swirling fur over his gun barrel," tumult and stillness were both his part:

> The earth faded to nothing. Only space and the game, the aim and the hunter. Mad emotions, powerful to rock worlds, hurled through the little man, but did not shake his tiniest nerve.
> When the rifle cracked, it shook his soul to a profound depth. Creation rocked and the bear stumbled.

Thus far, that is not unworthy of Faulkner or Hemingway in the same vein. But Crane was unable to rest in the romanticism either of them would have left dominating the sketch. Scrambling on the bear's trail, Crane's little man leaps for joy when he finds it dead, ". . . waving his hat as if he were leading the cheering of thousands. He ran up and kicked the ribs of the bear. Upon his face was the smile of the successful lover."

That same as yet slightly unfocused irony applies to the "clever Rudyard-Kipling style" of the sketches. It is a burlesque tone—the high style mocking low matter. In "The Octopush," for example, a drunken guide leaves the four fishermen marooned on stumps in a lake:

> A ghostlike mist came and hung upon the waters. The pond became a graveyard. The gray tree trunks and dark logs turned to monuments and crypts. Fireflies were wisp-lights dancing over graves, and then, taking regular shapes, appeared like brass nails in crude caskets. The [guide] . . . began to gibber. A gibber in a bass voice appalls the stoutest heart. It is the declamation of a genie. The little man began to sob; another groaned; and the two remaining, being timid by nature, swore great lurid oaths which blazed against the sky.

This easily became pseudo-biblical as well as pulpiteering and mock-William Jennings Bryan. When the guide did come near, "The little man kicked him. But the others cried out against him, so directly he left off." At its worst it could grate terribly on the ears, as in "The Cry of a Huckleberry Pudding," where the little man's stomach-ache incites "a howl that rolled and pealed.

. . . It clamored like a song of forgotten war, and died away to the screams of a maiden. The pleadings of fire-surrounded children mingled with the calls of wave-threatened sailors. Two barbarian tribes clashed together on a sunburnt plain; a score of barekneed clansmen crossed claymores amid gray rocks; a woman saw a lover fall; a dog was stabbed in an alley; a steel knight bit dust with bloody mouth. . . ."

Crane, hurried, distracted, or tired, would always be in danger of lapsing back toward that pompous style. It was a danger inherent in the conflict between his heroics and his irony. His intensity, as he well knew, was always liable to bathos. The careful student of the sources of his style will need to look to *The Bible,* to the schoolroom classics, and to pulpit style as well as to Kipling. But he would do well also to study the prevailing tones of the sports pages and of humor magazines like *Judge, Life* and *Puck.*

The largest significance of *The Sullivan County Sketches* may be, however, their recording so early and purely the meaning and weight to Crane the artist of the experience of Crane the sportsman. As we have seen, Crane from boyhood joined the sporting fraternity with "fiendish glee." He rode, hiked, hunted and camped, played baseball with a sacrificial passion, coached and played a bantam quarterback on a Jersey town football team in the fearsome days of massed interference and helping the runner. He pursued the mystery of manliness into the West as far as Mexico, on the filibuster *Commodore,* to Greece, and at last to Cuba.

It might be arguable that the trope basic to Crane's vision was that of the game. But the complexities of that vision to which he wished so desperately to be faithful were, to use one of his favorite words, immense. The trope is pervasive. He begins his serious efforts at fiction with hunting and camping sketches. The opening scene—and a governing symbol—of *Maggie* shows slum children viciously playing a favorite game: "King of the Hill." No few poems suggest that the procession of life is a game God plays with man, keeping the rules to Himself. The psychology, the whole essence of *The Red Badge of Courage,* Crane said he learned on the football field. As soon as he got to Greece and into combat he rejoiced that *The Red Badge* was all right–the "mental attitude" was right. And the war Crane saw was, repeatedly, "A Game"—as were his visions of *la hora de la verdad* in the West, Mexico, and Cuba.

For many reasons, however, the simpler ones being social, Crane was no Wister, Remington, nor Roosevelt. His vision was not only darker but deeper. Where they saw pain, struggle, and victory he saw agony and despair—at best tragedy. And above all, he saw irony. That irony could be wonderfully funny. One wonders why it is so seldom noticed, for instance, that "The Bride Comes to Yellow Sky" is a hilariously funny parody of neo-romantic lamentations over "The Passing of the West." The last marshal is tamed by a prosaic marriage and is ex- empted from playing The Game so absurdly romanticized by Street and Smith, *The Police Gazette*, and finally Owen Wister. His occupation gone, the last Bad Man, a part-time worker anyhow, shuffles off into the sunset dragging boot tracks through the dust like the tracks of the last dinosaur.

His experience of sports brought Crane knowledge, and at- titudes consequent on that knowledge, important to his point of view. It gave him the experience of testing his courage and thence his personal knowledge of pain and fear, victory and defeat. From that vantage point he commanded the cosmic gambler's stoic outlook: despising the petty, safe, and com- fortable; prizing the chance-taking, the enterprising, the seek- ing, aggressive and tough. In this respect he was at one with the prophets of the strenuous life. But he went beyond them in the depth of his forceful but ambivalent compassion for losers. He was anxious that their courage or at least their agony be defended against and registered upon the smug and ignorant. But he would not defend them against the law, against the rules of the game of life. It is because they express that compas- sion so magnificently, each differently from the other, that "The Open Boat" and "The Blue Hotel" are superior to, for instance, "Five White Mice," "A Man and Some Others," or "Horses—One Dash."

II

Whatever else it may be in actuality, *Maggie: A Girl of the Streets,* was clearly intended to be—and was afterwards under- stood by Crane to be—a work of realism. "I had no other purpose in writing 'Maggie' than to show people to people as they seem to me," he wrote in his oft-quoted letter to Miss Catherine Harris. "If that be evil, make the most of it."[3] This reflected Howells' definition of realism as "the truthful treatment of material" which Crane had picked up from Garland in 1891 and with which his post-Kipling creed was "identical." They all insisted that it did not mean being "photographic" but only, as Crane explained Garland explaining Howells, that "the novelist be true to himself and to things as he sees them."[4]

Crane's unspoken pact with Howells was the same Howells had with all the innumerable writers he helped. No discipleship was required, only honest development. Both sides were free to disagree without penalty so long as the amenities were observed, and between Howells and Crane they always were.[5] Crane grasped the essence of the idea of realism from the start in holding it to be a matter of seeing, a question of vision. In repeatedly stressing vision in moments of self-analysis, he proclaimed his continuous adherence to the doctrine. At mid-career, after *The Red Badge* had been written, Howells helped relieve Crane's poverty with a rare interview. Crane rewarded him with a presentation so uniquely clear among Howells' many explanations of realism that it becomes a major document. Presumably Crane had contributed substantially to incite if not guide the master.

Howells has been speaking of the "problem novel" and advising confinement of preaching to the pulpit. He continues:

"But it is the business of the novel—"
"Ah!" said the other man.
"It is the business of the novel to picture the daily life in the most exact terms possible, with an absolute and clear sense of proportion. That is the important matter—the proportion. As a usual thing, I think, people have absolutely no sense of proportion. Their noses are tight against life, you see. They perceive mountains where there are no mountains, but frequently a great peak appears no larger than a rat trap. An artist sees a dog down the street—well, his eye instantly relates the dog to its surroundings. The dog is proportioned to the buildings and the trees. Whereas, many people can conceive of that dog's tail resting upon a hilltop."
"You have often said that the novel is a perspective," observed the other man.
"A perspective, certainly. It is a perspective made for the

benefit of people who have no true use of their eyes. The novel, in its real meaning, adjusts the proportions. It preserves the balances. It is in this way that lessons are to be taught and reforms to be won. When people are introduced to each other they will see the resemblances, and won't want to fight so badly."

"I suppose that when a man tries to write 'what the people want'—when he tries to reflect the popular desire, it is a bad quarter of an hour for the laws of proportion."[6]

Supposing, as there is fair warrant for doing, that Crane somehow began *Maggie* in Syracuse and that it went through several drafts (Stallman guesses at four),[7] it is clear that the turn toward realism is what differentiates it from *The Sullivan County Sketches* both in style and "perspective." Perhaps Crane referred to that change in his inscription to Howells of "the veneration and gratitude of Stephen Crane for many things he has learned of the common man and, above all, for a certain readjustment of his point of view victoriously concluded some time in 1892."[8] With "point of view," the context becomes almost saturated with the realists' conjuring words.

Maggie: A Girl of the Streets is, then, a Bowery "perspective made for the benefit of people who have no true use of their eyes." And that seems the key to settling the problem of its "form."[9] Formally Crane's problem was a characteristically realistic or, indeed, Jamesian problem of perspective and proportion, of vision; and he solved it as well as he was able by the characteristic technique James called "scenes" and "pictures," habitually setting the action within the picture. Crane's numbered sections are significant of this technique, each having a kind of unity of its own. But they gather naturally into four major "perspectives," which one might label "A," "B," "C," and "D." The weakness of the *nouvelle's* structure is due precisely to the failure in proportion of what should have been the climactic one of these, "C."

Maggie starts effectively with three introductory sections. They begin with Jimmie Johnson squabbling raucously amid flying stones and Bowery objurgations to be "King of the Hill." Perspective "A" shows that he, Maggie, and little Tommie exist in a state of social and familial war and that their survival is dubious. The third section ends with the apparent drunken

murder of the father by the mother. Section IV and the beginning of Section V drop the "dramatic" method for a narrator's
swift foreshortening of intervening years in which Tommie dies;
Jimmie grows leather hard in aggression, egotism, and vice;
Mary (the mother) becomes an alcoholic, police-court dragon;
and Maggie blossoms "in a mud-puddle" and is rewarded with
a job in a sweatshop and romantic illusions about Jimmie's
friend, bartender Pete.

The major center, "B," of the tale goes scene-and-picture,
section after section, through the romance of Maggie and Pete,
with some foreshortening in description of the process by which
Maggie is wooed in Section VIII and some foreshadowing of the
end in XIII, from VI almost to the end of XVI. By that time
Maggie is "ruined" and gone "to the devil," has been deserted
by Pete, thrown out upon trying to go "home," and then thrown
out of the saloon by Pete. She wanders in aimless shock down
the street and discovers that her gait attracts men "with cal-
culating eyes." She drifts into a better neighborhood:

> Suddenly she came upon a stout gentleman in a silk hat and
> a chaste black coat, whose decorous row of buttons reached
> from his chin to his knees. The girl had heard of the grace
> of God and she decided to approach this man. His beaming,
> chubby face was a picture of benevolence and kind-heartedness.
> His eyes shone good will.
> But as the girl timidly accosted him he made a convulsive
> movement and saved his respectability by a vigorous side-step.
> He did not risk it to save a soul. For how was he to know that
> there was a soul before him that needed saving?[10]

That is a very effective bridge to what must now be perspective "C"—Maggie's downfall. Crane sketched it powerfully. He
did not paint, and he certainly did not dramatize it. He presented it in little more than a thousand words, even allowing
for the last, most sordid vignette he cut out between the first
and second editions. For this crucial Section XVII he reverted
to the earliest state of *Maggie*, when nobody had a name, and
she became simply "a girl of the painted cohorts of the city,"
soliciting. In swiftly telescoped moments she steps down and
down—compressing perhaps years as she goes: James D. McCabe
in *New York by Sunlight and Gaslight* (1882) estimated that it

took girls five to seven years to drop from the fashionable "first-class houses" through the scale to utter waterfront degradation and to death by disease, brutality, or the river. Maggie steps, handsomely dressed, daintily in "well-shod best" across "glittering avenues" in one paragraph to "the restless doors of saloons" in the next. Then a *boulevardier* turns her down because she is "neither new, Parisian or theatrical." Next in swift succession she descends past respectable, middle-class, and laboring men, past a careless boy, a drunk, "a man with blotched features," and at last "a ragged being with shifting, bloodshot eyes and grimy hands." Finally there is "the deathly black hue of the river. Some hidden factory sent up a yellow glare, that lit for a moment the waters lapping oilily against timbers. The varied sounds of life, made joyous by distance and seeming unapproachableness, came faintly and died away to a silence."

Thus Crane tells the sensitive reader what Jimmie will blurt at their mother, "Well, Mag's dead." But his way of telling the reader is, in the mere architectonics of the novel, not enough; its readers are not given time or enough weight of experience to register it properly. The suddenly sketchy mode of presentation is out of keeping with the tone and method of what precedes. Crane has perhaps done barely enough. His structure is not ruined. But it is not capped either. He is in danger of bathos.

He saved himself from that, however, with a return of powerful irony. It is double-barrelled. Pete, the betrayer, sits drunkenly in a saloon braying, "I'm a good f'ler. An' body trea's me right, I allus trea's 'em right!" while smart little whores fleece him. At "home" monstrous Mary Johnson stages a savage orgy of exhibitionistic mourning. The final words are: "She shook her great shoulders frantically, in an agony of grief. The tears seemed to scald her face. Finally her voice came and rose in a scream of pain. 'Oh, yes, I'll fergive her! I'll fergive her!' "[11]

The dialect in *Maggie* is thick as mud because it was so in the local color studies of the time and for the reasons Mark Twain advocated in "Fenimore Cooper's Literary Offences" and exemplified in *Huckleberry Finn*. Exactitude and density of representation in Bowery dialect, however, required profanity—and the suggestion of it—entirely too graphic for the magazine reader of the day who constituted the only market commercially worth having. Gilder, a friend of the family and later a Lanternite, declined *Maggie* for *The Century* for that among several reasons. And it was apparently the grand stumbling block in Howells' energetic and almost uniquely unsuccessful effort to get the book regularly published: "All its conscience and all its art could not save it," he lamented in mid-1895, "and it will probably remain unknown, but it embodied perhaps the best tough dialect which has yet found its way into print."[12] For the modern reader, as Howells had begun to suspect, that much dialect, while flavorful, seems too much of a good thing.

The succession of fine genre scenes stand as *Maggie's* clearest claim to be a triumph of realism. The tenement sketches, the kids and their street fights, the theater-saloon scenes, the wonderful bar fight in Pete's saloon all bear witness to the sharpness of that eye of Crane's. His long study of American low-life and the Bowery, with its aura of pride, pain, and revolt, paid off handsomely in *Maggie* as in *George's Mother*. But to make this statement raises the question of Crane's "sources" in this first and, after all the debits have been entered, marvelously successful prentice work.

Obviously, writing literature is a process culturally determined in large degree, and learning to do it is learning from other writers until one has achieved his own mastery—and so buckets of ink have been spread in the tracing of literary "influences"— and often foolishly. When dealing with an achieved work of art and not a plagiarism or a derivation (a bad copy), the best situation for "influence study" is that in which Writer X can be proved to have written Book B after reading Book A by Writer Y. It will be possible to show that portions of B resemble A. What will that prove? What are the facts useful for? Primarily they are useful in helping to read B better. The facts don't on their face prove anything; for it may easily be as true that X exploits Y because, in Emersonian or Melvillean fashion, Y happens to suit X's mood and needs as that X's book became what it was because he somehow discovered his creative impulse in Y—which last is the assumption usual to "influence" studies.

There are two schools of thought, neither in itself necessary, about the "sources" for *Maggie*. The oldest and most natural was that which Crane so resented in British *littérateurs*: he had "stolen" from some French naturalist. In the case of *Maggie*, as Frank Norris noted at once, it must have been Zola and

L'Assommoir.[13] Marcus Cunliffe, on the contrary, notes that
there was a well-established American tradition of minatory
literature and sermons concerning prostitution and slum-life.[14]
He might have added McCabe's sort of guidebook volume and
an entire tradition of soap-operatic, Richardsonian seduction
novels. And then, of course, there were the many levels, other
than reading, of Crane's experience: his merciful father's concern for sinners; the lady cousin whose book was condemned
by *The Nation* in 1871 for dealing with but being insufficiently
punitive of New York prostitution.[15] His moral, religious, and
social ambivalences were likewise "sources" in what must have
been for him (as for every artist) a *gestalt* of provenience far
more complex than the "influence" study allows.

No effort thus far to show *Maggie* as "symbolistic" merits
attention, but there can be no doubt that the perspectives of the
novel were aimed at something tendentious. Crane's ideas were
dramatized for the reader to reflect upon, not spoken out. This
was the "unmoralized morality" which Howells in praising
James had distinguished as one of the hallmarks of the new
fiction, but it was there. Shaken by his own defiance in printing
his book in the teeth of a disapproving world, Crane developed
a little message which he inscribed across the yellow faces of his
paperbacked volumes. The one to Hamlin Garland is typical:

> It is inevitable that you be greatly shocked by this book but
> continue, please, with all possible courage to the end. For it
> tries to show that environment is a tremendous thing in the world
> and frequently shapes lives regardless. If one proves that theory
> one makes room in Heaven for all sorts of souls (notably an
> occasional street girl) who are not confidently expected to be
> there by many excellent people.
>
> It is probable that the reader of this small thing may consider
> the Author to be a bad man, but, obviously, this is of small
> consequence to
> The Author[16]

Writing about slums and their brutality and about a prostitute,
concerned about environment and excusing what society calls
sin by appeal to the power of environment, was Crane in *Maggie*
not "a naturalist"? The epithet has often been attached to book
and author, but it is by no means clear what is meant by it.
Some careful students of "literary naturalism" have ended in

despair, concluding that it is impossible to know what the word means. This is a state familiar to every investigator of large terms—for example, "romanticism," or "the baroque."

The latest systematic consideration of the subject is Charles Child Walcutt's *American Literary Naturalism, A Divided Stream* (1956), which begins quite justifiably with a cautious notation of "the Protean slipperiness" of the problem and a method of approach which surrounds more than it defines "naturalism." When Walcutt comes to "Stephen Crane: Naturalist and Impressionist," however, one feels at first that Proteus has been firmly grasped. Crane's "works" are called "an early and unique flowering of pure naturalism." But in the next breath Proteus squirms loose and begins to shift his shape from sentence to sentence: "It is naturalism in a restricted and special sense, and it contains many non-naturalistic elements, but it is nevertheless entirely consistent and coherent. It marks the first entry, in America, of a deterministic philosophy not confused with ethical motivation into the structure of the novel. Ethical judgement there is in plenty" (66).

This seems a confusing statement. Walcutt holds that Crane must be "naturalistic" because "nowhere does a character operate as a genuinely free ethical agent in defiance of the author's intentions" (67). By "free ethical agent," as the chapter develops, he appears to mean one who makes moral choices free of all contingency. Theologians have doubted that God possesses such freedom (He is conditioned by Himself). Certainly no one ever supposed that any human being had such freedom—and, if one did suppose so, it would obviously be impossible to write a novel about the libertine. Crane's "intentions" are taken for granted as proved by what the critic finds in the text, and his "frantic impressionism" (70) is undefined as "ism" and illustrated as "frantic," even insane, by quotations from Mary Johnson's spree scenes.

"The impressions that these people are not free agents, and that their freedom is limited as much by their conventional beliefs as by their poverty, are naturalistic concepts completely absorbed into the form of the story," says Walcutt (69). By this he means that Crane is the complete naturalistic artist, "the Christopher Marlowe of American naturalism—and we have had no Shakespeare" (67). It is necessary to dwell on Professor

Walcutt because his is the most authoritative plea for a reading
of Crane as naturalist, but one must say that his case is not
proven—or probable. There is not really in *Maggie* either the
naturalism of Walcutt or "the cold-blooded determinism of . . .
belief" which Spiller saw in Crane.[17]

The issue is best joined over the emphases in Walcutt's analysis
of *Maggie*: most of it falls on the first few sections of the book;
and no note at all is taken of the terrible ironies of the final two
sections except to quote the last lines as "this classic paragraph."
It was Crane's *donnée* that the flower of a Maggie who "blos-
somed in a mud puddle" should be spiritually as well as physically beautiful: innocent and vulnerable in spite of her environment. Nothing could be less "natural" or, indeed, realistic. It
was part of the chivalrous anachronism about women which
Crane shared with Twain, Howells, and James, among the
realists. But it was his *donnée*. She is trapped by the environment *in toto*, of which other people are a part. Crane never
suggests that there is excuse for the others—or "room in Heaven"
for Jimmie or Pete, or especially Mary.

They may not have been wholly "free," but all three of
Maggie's antagonists—Mary persuading Jimmie (XIII), and
Pete (XVI)—do literally make ethical choices which damn her.
She is "trun' out" to "go to th' devil," and she does as she must.
Of course Crane is assailing the conventional morality of Rum
Alley with the ironies of Pete's maudlin "good f'ler" protestations
and Mary's unbearable "fergiveness." But any reader who con-
gratulates himself that moral obtuseness and arrogance are
confined to Rum Alley is incautious. He is dealing with a writer
whom intimations of naturalism had reached, nobody knows
how. But he is also dealing with an outraged Christian in agonies
of doubt and rebellion against the pious smugness of non-
Christian conventionalities. In *Maggie* there are also the mis-
sionary who never says "we" to the Bowery but always "you
are damned," and the roseate, skipping bishop.

Today's sexually more permissive age has by no means ceased
casting stones to the destruction of prostitutes. And even if it
should, the basically ethical and humane questions of sin, guilt,
complicity, and condemnation would remain. Crane's young
irony came from no such inured *saeva indignatio* as Swift's. But
real moral passion burned behind it. The early achievement of

the style; the realistic power of scene and picture; the historical accuracy of speech, setting and type; and the historical defiance of the genteel censors would all lend *Maggie* importance if there were nothing else.

There may be something, or not, in all that which need be called "naturalistic." What gives the little book living importance is the moral vitality of its irony. And that is not the self-pitying irony of the naturalist which says, in effect, man dreamed he was human, perhaps even divine, but he is only an animal: how pitiful! Crane's irony mocks and scalds as irony should. Then, in *Maggie* it points to a morality of concern, of human warmth and humility, of acknowledged complicity like that of Hawthorne or Melville's Ishmael or, indeed, of Howells.

Jimmie, Pete, and Mary are at last the conceited cowards (not the naturalistic victims) Crane found typical of the slums and Bowery. Maggie, however, was by definition an innocent. Of such Crane wrote Miss Harris, "The missions for children are another thing and if you will have Mr. Rockefeller give me a hundred street cars and some money I will load all the babes off to some pink world where cows can lick their noses and they will never see their families any more." Perhaps Crane believed no more literally in "Heaven for all sorts of souls (notably an occasional street girl)" than in a "pink world." But there is no evidence to show that he had definitively settled the question in a naturalistically acceptable way or that his literature should be read as if he had.

III

On the contrary, his next book, *The Black Riders*, immensely complicates the notion of any sort of settlement. It was wholly other than realistic, and the poems set Howells to grumbling about a waste of Crane's time and talents. It was free verse, strikingly imagistic, and masculine in a total rejection of Tennysonian euphonies. Perhaps it was symbolistic, perhaps not—it was hard to tell. Any reader could tell that the poet was earnestly engaged with ideas even if he did not know that the poet had insisted to the publisher that he not "cut all the ethical sense out of the book. All the anarchy, perhaps. It is the anarchy which I particularly insist upon. . . . The ones which refer to God . . . I am obliged to have. . . ."[18] Hoffman has summed up the sense of these key poems in his heading for a chapter interpreting them: "War in Heaven."

No naturalist, much less a "pure" one, could have taken the idea of the reality of God seriously. There is no doubt that Crane, while of several minds and consciously "anarchical" (the worst kind of revolutionary in the popular mind of the day), was serious. One critic has drawn extended parallels between *The Black Riders* and John Bunyan's masterpiece.[19] Young, semi-educated, a preacher's son, and unaccustomed to discussing ideas, Crane doubtless exaggerated the "anarchy" of his position. Indeed, if he had been more *au courant*, he might have lapsed into the conspiracy of skeptical silence of the polite. As it was, he cared too much.

Except, as must always be the case with explications, for a wish to read some poems a little differently from the way he does, one can scarcely improve on Hoffman's "War in Heaven" chapter. It is in many ways the heart of his admirable achievement in *The Poetry of Stephen Crane*. The religious attitudes, and Hoffman's convincing inferences as to their provenience, of Crane's poems we have already summarized. But it may be useful to quote representatively.

Sometimes Crane imagined in accord with a naturalistic sense of reality:

LXVI

If I should cast off this tattered coat,
And go free into the mighty sky;
If I should find nothing there
But a vast blue,
Echoless, ignorant—
What then?

But again a truly Calvinistic imagination responds:

LXVIII

A spirit sped
Through spaces of night;
And as he sped, he called,
"God! God!"
He went through valleys
Of black death-slime,

> Ever calling,
> "God! God!"
> Their echoes
> From crevice and cavern
> Mocked him:
> "God! God! God!"
> Fleetly into the plains of space
> He went, ever calling,
> "God! God!"
> Eventually, then, he screamed,
> Mad in denial,
> "Ah, there is no God!"
> A swift hand,
> A sword from the sky,
> Smote him,
> And he was dead.

Crane had, however, no idea of being intimidated by that awful Jehovah. "Well, then, I hate Thee, unrighteous picture" (XII), he informed the Old Testament God who visited the sins of the fathers upon the heads of the children. But he also knew a "God of his inner thoughts" who

> . . . looked at him
> With soft eyes
> Lit with infinite comprehension
> And said, "My poor child!"
> (LI)

For the blustering Bully Jehovah, he was quick to express contempt:

> Withal there is One whom I fear;
> I fear to see grief upon that face.
> Perchance, friend, He is not your God;
> If so, spit upon Him.
> By it you will do no profanity.
> But I—
> Ah, sooner would I die
> Than see tears in those eyes of my soul.
> (LIII)

Though there was much in *The Black Riders* not dreamt of in the philosophy of *Le Roman expérimental*, or of *Criticism and*

Fiction, that says nothing of the quality as poetry of these and the rest of Crane's "lines," "pills," or what not, as he called them to evade the sissy soubriquet of "poet." They constitute a perfectly personal expression, defying categorization; they are much more difficult to paraphrase than they seem until one tries; at their best, they are extraordinarily subtle in phonetic effect. One can find analogues, but no true sources for them as poems. To be sure they are "Biblical" and have predecessors in the wisdom literature of the ages—or the pseudo-wisdom literature of Crane's age. But there are no poems like these: Crane, by not trying to be a poet, achieved a genuinely organic expression of the religious, moral, amatory, the nature-loving, and particularly the ironic experiences rioting through his head.

The result was above all intense. Taking the best of Crane's poetry from all volumes (and one judges poets first and last by their best), the imagery is unforgettable. The power of definition is as illuminating as Emily Dickinson's. The sharp, often agonizingly ironic parables are dramatic, with a symbolism often almost surrealistically extreme, yet humane—and available to our common experience—too:

> The wayfarer,
> Perceiving the pathway to truth,
> Was struck with astonishment.
> It was thickly grown with weeds.
> "Ha," he said,
> "I see that none has passed here
> "In a long time."
> Later he saw that each weed
> Was a singular knife.
> "Well," he mumbled at last,
> "Doubtless there are other roads."[20]

Of course Crane is not a major poet. He had neither a sustained poetic career nor any apparent desire for one. Sometimes his imagination paid out an unexpected poetic dividend while he lived for fiction. Nevertheless, as he was aware, these were his most personal, intimately revealing expressions. There are perhaps twenty of them to make up a body of perfectly genuine, wholly successful and individual, and extraordinarily intense poetry.

[114]

The Red Badge of Courage

IN A WAY one could say that *The Red Badge of Courage*, Crane's masterpiece, was built of the romantic irony of the sketches, plus, the complicit irony of *Maggie*, plus the imagistic fire of the poems, plus Crane's unexpectedly gifted historical imagination, plus his life-long intimations of war, plus a new heightening of his artistic powers and perceptions. But saying so, one would not have covered the ground—only have suggested some of the approaches to a work which has "made" all sorts of lists of "classics," sold fabulously (to whose enrichment?), and engendered, comparatively recently, a curiously embattled and inconsistent body of criticism.

Since 1945 there have been perhaps twenty-five significant critiques of the novel, including an interesting and useful case-book edited by Lettis and others. Something is revealed, one fears, about the scope, persistence, and courage of the oft-vaunted "modern criticism" that among these there has been no thorough, comprehensive, formal explication and evaluation of the whole book. Most are admittedly fragmentary or partial, and the best are demonstrably incomplete. One of the conclusions suggested by a survey of Crane criticism generally, in fact, is that the lessons of the latterly New Criticism have been badly learned. Instead of a responsible, "serious" criticism, there has been in many instances a self-indulgent literary comment essentially frivolous—apparently because it supposes that the teaching of the New Criticism was to throw off, along with obsolescent academic ponderosities, all responsibility to the ordinary intellectual disciplines of logic, evidence, materiality, and relevance.

As other critics have demonstrated, much of this "criticism" will not meet the simplest tests of contextuality (one should be able to find warrant for what he "discovers" about the work in the fair context of the actual words of the text); coherence (the patterns discovered should make coherent sense in themselves, unless it is to be shown that the work is incoherent); and completeness (the interpretation should take cognizance of all the work and apply to all of it, not just some convenient fragment). The problem is by no means unique to Crane criticism, but for some critics self-validating intuition seems to replace a sense of responsibility to common, market-place communication. One would think they were the artists. The resultant warfare has not been, however, without value; and some recent commentary has considerably cleared the atmosphere, notably that by Colvert, Friedman, Greenfield, Liebling, Mordecai Marcus, and Solomon (see bibliography).

The problems to which Crane criticism has addressed itself are the traditionary ones: Provenience—what are the sources of Crane's inspiration? Method—is the novel symbolistic, naturalistic, impressionistic, realistic, or something else, and how successful is it as art? Meaning—what is the substance of the ideas presented or implied, and how does one prove his reading of them by solving the problems of structure, irony, and conclusion?

I

To match the literature which insists that Shakespeare must have been a lawyer to sketch Shallow, there has always been amateurish Road-to-Xanaduing about *The Red Badge of Courage.* The logic of the search is simple. Crane wrote impressively about war but hadn't seen any; he must have borrowed from other literature. As with *Maggie,* Continental "sources" have been popular, especially Zola's *La Débâcle* and Tolstoy's *War and Peace* or *Sebastopol,* despite Joseph Conrad's trenchant judgment: "I could not see the relevancy."[1] Almost any book about a lad who goes to war will do. There is, therefore, also a small school of discoverers of American sources which have been nominated:[2] Hinman, *Corporal Si Klegg and His 'Pard'* (1887); Joseph Kirkland, *The Captain of Company K* (1891); Murford, *The Coward: A Novel of Society and the Field in 1863* (1863); Armstrong, *Red-Tape and Pigeon-Hole Generals* (1864). Others, like *All Quiet on the Rappahannock,* have been ignored. The real point seems to be that there was a general—indeed, a rather homogenized—and certainly sub-literary tradition of semi-fictional Civil War memorials behind Crane's tale. He may have had them in mind when he first thought of his pot-boiler. But there is no reliable evidence that he had read any book about war other than *Battles and Leaders* before he wrote *The Red Badge*.

Much the same is true of guesses about where Crane got his title. Could it have been from Shakespeare's "Murder's crimson badge" in *Henry VI*—or is that a remote coincidence? Or was it from the red shoulder patch New Jersey's glamorous General Phil Kearney invented for his Third Corps?[3] Well, possibly, but in the Barrett manuscript, it is clear that Crane first called the novel "Private Fleming His Various Battles." He crossed that out and substituted the provocative, classic title apparently at the same time he went through the text cancelling the names of the soldiers wherever he could and abstracting them into "the tall soldier," "the loud soldier," "the youth," etc. In thinking back over his novel, Crane had had plenty of time to reflect upon his own phrase from Chapter Six, where deserter Fleming among the wounded "wished that he, too, had a wound, a little red badge of courage"—a "blighty" the Tommies called it in World War I because it sent them home a while with honor—and upon the pivotal irony of the unplanned fraudulence with which Fleming received the scalp wound, the necessary badge to let him back to his platoon with impunity.

No little of the source hunting, or of Crane "scholarship" generally, suffers from an impression like that of Harvey Wickham's assurance that *George's Mother* was studied from Wickham's own very respectable relatives because "Frank" was seen by Crane to eat "George's amazing lunch—charlotte russe and a beer."[4] That would be dubious proof of the allegation at best. Unfortunately, it happens that "a Charlotte Russe and a glass of beer" was never George's lunch. It was the unpalatable offering of the equally unpalatable "Bowery jay" who tried to pick Maggie up after her first betrayal by Pete.[5]

Granting the sophistication necessary to have written what preceded *The Red Badge*, it is not clear that Crane had to have literary "sources." Obviously he had been fascinated by "Claverack's student batallion . . .the nucleus of that 'blue demonstration,' the very heart of his subsequent conception of an army."[6]

His boyhood could scarcely have avoided middle-aged Grand Army of the Republic veterans, who were often as garrulous as they were ubiquitous in the 1880's. And Stephen would hardly have wished not to learn all he could of war from men who had been there. The most conspicuous of these was Crane's history teacher at Claverack, the "Reverend General" John B. Van Petten. He had advanced from chaplain to field officer in years of combat experience during the Civil War and been mustered out a brigadier. At Fair Oaks, Antietam, and Winchester he had seen not only hard fighting but many of the types of incidents used in *The Red Badge*. His after-dinner reminiscenses may well have supplied the emotional, psychological coloring Crane indignantly missed from *Battles and Leaders*. In any case, Van Petten abundantly illustrates the oral traditions, the substance from the climate of his youth, which, with his personal concern for war, fear, and courage in life, would have been sufficient "source" for Crane had there been no other.[7]

II

It has been variously asserted that Crane's way of imagining and constructing *The Red Badge of Courage* was realist, naturalist, impressionist, or symbolist. It would make a difference if it could be demonstrated that one of them, or any other, was *the* method. One would then expect to interpret particular parts, and the whole, in certain ways, and one's reading and response would be affected accordingly. But the conviction with which these various views have been urged by sensitive and intelligent critics might in itself warn the reader that no unitary view is exclusively right. The very secret of the novel's power inheres in the inviolably organic uniqueness with which Crane adapted all four methods to his need. *The Red Badge's* method is all and none. There is no previous fiction like it.

The narrative point of view, however, is nothing new. James and Howells had been developing the technique used in *The Red Badge* for years; they repeatedly displayed it with an easy virtuosity which Crane could hardly have missed in the big magazines. In the earliest pages of *The Red Badge*, the storyteller's point of view, the narrative line-of-sight along events which will afford the readers' perspective, is permanently estab-

lished. The voice is that of a third-person, "objective" narrator—
not a first-person, "subjective" teller who says "Call me Ishmael"
or "You don't know me without you have read a book. . . ."
But the point of view is located at almost the same place as
if this were a first-person narrative: it is just behind the eyes of
"the youthful private." The reader sees through Henry Fleming's
eyes, and he is able to reflect backwards somewhat to record
what goes on in Henry's mind (though never, of course, to
overhear his "stream of consciousness"). But for the most part
the reader is limited to seeing and hearing the life of the fiction
as the narrator does; he can never "go behind" into the mind
of another character.

These limitations make the experience afforded by the novel
seem objective and thus credible, very intense, yet also somewhat
detached and impersonal. The reader is not invited to "identify"
wholly with young Fleming—a fact Joseph Hergesheimer recalled mourning over in his youth.[8] Fleming is part of a drama.
He is to be subject to criticism, to judgment unintrusively unmoralized, established dramatically and ironically, but forcefully
there. Essentially this is a perspective—but upon what? And to
what end? What finally is the force of its proportion, its total
form?

One way to begin to answer these questions is to notice some
distinctions about the problem of point of view in this or any
modern fiction which have not always been observed in discussing The Red Badge. At least four classes of "point of view"
function in fiction. In simplest forms these are the author's, as
he imagines and builds the work; the narrator's, which in any
sophisticated fiction is not the author's way of looking at his
work but an instrument of his technique in presenting it; the
character's (or characters'), in the interplay of which—with one
another and the narrator's viewpoints—lies a great deal of the
craftsman's resource; and, finally, the reader's. Author's and
reader's points of view are external to the novel. It may turn
out that the reader's has been very skillfully played upon by the
author who uses as instruments the internal points of view of
narrator and characters.

The distinction in The Red Badge of Courage between the
narrator's point of view and that of Henry Fleming, the sole
character's view which the reader knows at all directly, is subtle

for the reason already suggested. The narrator's point of view is through Fleming's eyes. But though the reader sees what and as Fleming does, the reader is not he. (Henry's point of view is that of his own experience; the reader knows it as, with the narrator, he goes reflexively "behind" for reports on that experience.)

Material for observation of all this experience is very rich in the first four or five pages of the novel. It starts with a swiftly telescoped atmospheric registering of the context. Morning and early spring are telescoped in the first sentence:

> The cold passed reluctantly from the earth, and the retiring fogs revealed an army stretched out on the hills, resting. As the landscape changed from brown to green, the army awakened, and began to tremble with eagerness at the noise of rumors. It cast its eyes upon the roads, which were growing from the long troughs of liquid mud to proper thoroughfares. A river, amber-tinted in the shadow of its banks, purled at the army's feet; and at night, when the stream had become of a sorrowful blackness, one could see across it the red, eye-like gleam of hostile camp-fires set in the low brows of distant hills.

It might, parenthetically, be possible to argue that the foregoing "one could see" establishes a narrative point of view distinct from Fleming's. But such an argument is unnecessarily messy and less than appreciative of Crane's artistic achievement. He handles point of view more like a movie camera than perhaps any predecessor had done. The reader stands to see somewhere back of Fleming's eyes. Sometimes the reader gets the long "panning" shot, sometimes the view only Henry could see, sometimes an interior view limited only by Crane's ignorance of methods Joyce would discover.

So the reader moves at once to a spirited, comic camp scene as tall Jim Conklin falsely reports imminent action. Then he retires with Fleming to ponder his emotions "in a little trance of astonishment" within the security of his hut. And suddenly his memory flashes back to the scenes and thoughts of his enlistment at home months before. It is the content of that flashback—seen by the reader through the narrator's double perception of what Fleming's point of view is now and what it was earlier—that presents the basic problem of the novel.

The reader begins, then, with a perspective upon the perspectives of "the youth." They go back to dreams of battle and personal magnificence in war, dreams he has classed with "thought-images of heavy crowns and high castles"—the cloudy symbols of a high romance. Awake, this adolescent Minniver Cheevy "had long despaired of witnessing a Greek-like struggle. Such would be no more, he said. Men were better, or more timid. Secular and religious education had effaced the throat-grappling instinct, or else firm finance held in check the passions." On the farm, Fleming was a perfect neo-romantic.

Tales of "the war in his own country" inevitably began to move him, however. "They might not be distinctly Homeric, but there seemed to be much glory in them." In the face of his mother's Christian pacifism and her quietly effective ironic undercutting of his egotism, he eventually enlisted and left for camp with a soaring conviction "that he must be a hero." But the monotonous realities of camp life had taught him to concentrate on personal comfort and retreat "back to his old ideas. Greek-like struggles would be no more." Now, perhaps on the edge of the real thing, new possibilities of truth emerge. Maybe he will be a coward! "He felt that in this crisis his laws of life were useless. Whatever he had learned of himself was here of no avail. He was an unknown quantity. He saw that he would again be obliged to experiment as he had in early youth." When it turned out that the battle was not on the morrow, he had days to make "ceaseless calculations . . . all wondrously unsatisfactory." Examination of self and scrutiny of others were defeated. Only experience would help: "to go into the blaze, and then figuratively to watch his legs to discover their merits and faults . . . he must have blaze, blood, and danger, even as a chemist requires this, that and the other."

Except for the initial paragraph, the method and issues so far established are those of the realists. The emphasis on point of view, on vision, is theirs; and the establishment of a problem of knowledge, which will require an exercise in discovery and revelation, is theirs. So, too, is the pragmatic dependence on experience: answering the question by watching whether one's legs ran or stayed might have come straight from James's *Principles of Psychology*. And raising the issues of romanticism—the heroic, the glamorous, the egotistical, exalted and sentimental—was a confirmed habit of the realists. Anti-romanticism, the reduction by ridicule and irony of the romantic to the common, negative realism, was the first and always the easiest way for the realists to define themselves. Positive realism, finding the beauty, power, and meaning of life in the commonplace— a green farm boy among his peers in an unblooded regiment, for instance—was much more difficult. But the wrangling amateur military experts in the company street and the soldiers' hut are scenically presented—they talk and act—with a humorous precision dear to the heart of any lover of the common American man.

III

One does not read far into *The Red Badge of Courage*, however, without discovering that it is very different from the traditional realistic novel. The extended and massive specification of detail with which the realist seems to impose upon one an illusion of the world of the common vision is wholly missing. Equally absent is the tremendous procession of natural and social "forces" characteristic of naturalism—of Frank Norris or Dreiser trying to be Zola. Detail is not absent, but it is comparatively sparingly deployed on a light, mobile structure; and it is used for intensive, not extensive effects. Reference to "forces" is there, but no effort at all to show them streaming in their mighty currents, floating the characters as tracers, as chips on the stream whose significance is to reveal the trending of the currents.

One of the more reliable ways, indeed, to distinguish romantic from realistic and both from naturalistic fiction is to examine the way each handles its characters. To the romancer the significance of his people is symbolic; they are representative men and women who reveal, by the doctrine of correspondence, spiritual truths (*viz.*, Chingachgook, Chillingworth, Goodman Brown, Captain Ahab and all his men). The reductive, agnostic realist, however, cannot believe in the spiritual sublimity, the ideality, of his characters. He levels his vision to the human, fascinated by the paradoxes of the common person: his individuality, his commonplace mediocrity, the representative, perhaps universal, meaning of his "common" moral problems. To the naturalist, finally, humanity means only animality. This is the ultimate reduction. Where the romancer's concern was superhuman and the realist's humane, the naturalist's is infrahuman. And in a sense the naturalist joins hands with the romancer (no matter how the latter might cringe) again in looking not so much to what the man is as to what he can be made to reveal about realities far larger, stronger, more important and more abstract than man.

In this intent, too, Crane stands with the realists, but he stands historically in advance of them toward the coming future of the novel. The critics of his own day who wondered if Crane did not represent a "new realism" may have been more than a little right.[9] It was natural, if not inevitable, that the realism of the generation previous to Crane should develop to prepare the way for its own displacement. The shift was toward an increasingly psychological realism, and it was propelled by at least two major forces. One of these was the displacement of positivism from its dominance of late nineteenth-century thought. A decade like the 1890's, which began with William James's *Psychology* and ended with the unleashing of the new, electronic factors in physics which produced Henry Adams' image of "himself lying in the Gallery of Machines at the Great Exposition of 1900, his historical neck broken by the sudden irruption of forces totally new," was bound at the least to loosen the grip of positivism on the imagination. The second force, however, arose from the practice of realistic fiction itself. The more one confronted the mystery of men as persons living out their fates and struggling toward their deaths, the more one's scrutiny turned from the outward sign to the inward process itself. Howells noticed in 1903, when he was writing a novel Freudian in all but specifically Viennese terminology for the main concept, that all the realists had of late been turning to psychology. Indeed, many of them had been flirting with psychic phenomena as far-flung as the claims of spiritualism. What he did not seem to notice was that he himself had been working largely in psychological realism since *The Shadow of a Dream* in 1891.

For the better part of thirty-five years, Howells had fought at the foremost point in a great battle to capture American taste for realism. He had defined realism as the objective truth in art about the visible aspects of human life. But in 1903 he registered his realization that a change had occurred among the great realists of the world. God seems to love the game of the pendulum in man's affairs, he observed. And now "A whole order of literature has arisen, calling itself psychological, as realism called itself scientific . . . it is not less evident in Tolstoi, in Gorky, in Ibsen, in Björnsen, in Hauptmann, and in Mr. Henry James, than in Maeterlinck himself."[10]

It was like Howells to leave himself out of the account. The surprising thing is his so registering the change almost fifteen years after he had launched himself into it. What he apparently did not see was that what he called "the present psychologism" was not just a providential swing of the pendulum but a fairly predictable outcome of the earlier realism–and that it was already bridging the way for the interior, stream of consciousness, and therefore symbolic fiction which would succeed it. The realism of which Howells had been the chief American prophet had been, as he said, "scientific" in the mid-nineteenth century sense of factualistic and "objective." It had also been intensely humanistic, fixing its focus on persons, on characters, in their human dimensions, qualities, conflicts, problems, and fates. The more it fastened on characters and the visible evidence of inner conditions, the more that realism would be tempted to "go behind" as James said. The further behind the veil of sense it went, the less normally and normatively visible its evidences would be. After a while it would no longer be the realist's appeal to the common vision which would win the reader's suspension of disbelief, but only a faith in the realist's honesty of covert vision secured, perhaps, by his faithfulness to that common vision in overt matters. The turn to psychology opened important and exciting vistas to the accomplished realist like Henry James. It also paved the way for the displacement of realism by such masters to come as Joyce, Anderson, Lawrence, and Faulkner.

The Red Badge of Courage was the first masterpiece of that transition, as Howells imperfectly saw while reviewing it. Most commendable, he said, was "the skill shown in evolving from the youth's crude expectations and ambitions a quiet honesty and self-possession manlier and nobler than any heroism had imagined . . . and decidedly on the psychological side the book is worth while as an earnest of the greater things that we may hope for from a new talent working upon a high level, not quite clearly as yet, but strenuously."[11] In a lifetime devoted to part-time criticism, Howells had a high batting average, but this time he hit only a part of the ball. He may have been told or have divined Crane's interest in the psychological. Crane was able to be overt about it from Greece, telling John Bass that "Between two great armies battling against each other the interesting thing is the mental attitude of the men." Or, as he explained himself to his English readers, people "think they ought to demand" of "descriptions of battle" that they be placed "to stand in front of the mercury of war and see it rise or fall . . . but it is an absurd thing for a writer to do if he wishes to reflect, in any way, the mental condition of the men in the ranks. . . ."[12]

"To reflect . . . the mental condition of the men in the ranks," representing them especially with one youth, is an exact definition of the achievement—and probably the intention—of *The Red Badge of Courage*. Its formal structure is rather simply Aristotelian. It has a beginning (Chapters I-IV), which gets the youth to real battle; a middle (Chapters V-XIII), which witnesses his runaway and return; and an end (Chapters XIV-XXIII), which displays his achievement of "heroism" at climax, followed by a certain understanding of it in a coda-like final chapter. The middle and end sections are replete with notations of Fleming's psychological responses to fear, stress, and courage. There are progressively at least ninety such notations of Fleming's state of nerves-mind-psyche (it is not at all clear that Crane had any coherent psychological theory to exploit). They occur in pairs or triads of alternating or developmental stages as well as singly and are sometimes recurrent. If only by mere weight, the ninety constitute a major part of the substance of a short novel.

Actually, of course, psychological notations count for far more than mere bulk in *The Red Badge*. They are fascinating in themselves. For instance, Crane recorded something he no doubt picked up from football (as psychologists are said to have done later, naming the phenomenon "scrimmage blackout"). In the depth of combat, Crane supposed, Fleming would pass into an absorptive trance in which he was conscious of little but performed with intense automatism in a "battle-sleep" during which he might occasionally "dream" impressions. Essential to the achievement of the novel are the psychological patterns Crane divined for Fleming's combat experience. One is the obverse of the other. In the one, fear leads to panic, panic to guilt, guilt to rationalization and eventually to frustration and acquiescence. In the other, resentment produces rage, and rage "battle sleep"; resolution, including willingness to die, follows and leads in turn to "heroism" and at last to adumbrations of emotional realism and modesty. Equally striking are Crane's observations of the complexities of individual-group relations.

If this psychologism carried Crane past realism, it also defined his sense of naturalism, at least for this novel. Philosophic naturalism in *The Red Badge of Courage* is used, not expounded. It is identified as a form of romanticism, a buttress to the ego, a means of escape from moral reality and responsibility. In the end it is rejected. It is referred to—in the final state of the novel more obliquely than directly—so often as to leave little doubt that Crane was quite aware of its patterns of explanation and their potential uses. But it is at last only a foil for the pragmatic, relativistic ideas toward which the novel finally points.

It may also indicate Crane's decision about naturalism at this point to note that he cut most of the explicit references to its ideas out of *The Red Badge* at various stages of revision. No thorough collation of all the states of the emergent text of the novel has ever been published; and one is badly needed. But examination of the Barrett manuscript tends to confirm Professor Stallman's steps toward a variorium text[13] in *A Stephen Crane Omnibus*. Contrary to the notion that Crane never revised, one can work out at least seven states of *The Red Badge* text. Without knowing what preceded the text which Crane's poverty preserved in cancelled fragments on the versos of a later state, one starts with the earliest extant draft which Stallman labelled "SV." Next, presumably comes the Bacheller syndicated text (which may have been excised from "SV"), then the extant manuscript (Stallman's "LV") which stands in four states, having been revised in pen, in pencil, and finally in blue crayon. Before the first edition, there was a lost typescript revised nobody knows how often.

Rather boldly explicit in draft but variously suppressed and left implicit in the final text was Crane's association of philosophic naturalism with Henry Fleming's panic syndrome. One may guess that he thought to make the resultant theme central to the novel's development and then changed his mind.

Early in the morning of his first battle day, Fleming dashes, wild with curiosity, upon the scene of what he expects will be immediate combat. But it is bathos, nothing really is happening; and as the regiment presses on into a silently ominous landscape, his courage oozes away: "This advance upon Nature was too calm . . . absurd ideas took hold upon him. . . . It was all a trap." With this comes the idea associated throughout: he must become a prophet of the truth "Nature" reveals. "He thought that he must break from the ranks and harangue his comrades. . . . The generals were idiots. . . . There was but one pair of eyes in the corps." But fear of ridicule silences him as the tense ranks advance "to look at war, the red animal—war, the blood-swollen god."[14] However, nature is no constant for Fleming; she varies with his psychic states. After his first and successful combat, he wakes from his battle-sleep with "a flash of astonishment at the blue pure sky and the sun gleaming on the trees and fields. It was surprising that Nature had gone tranquilly on with her golden process in the midst of so much devilment."[15]

Fleming's later efforts to appeal to nature as a constant and as a source of comforting revelation (or rationalization) are therefore doomed. If one were to argue from *The Red Badge of Courage* about Crane's attitudes toward the naturalistic argument for man's animal irresponsibility toward duty and morality he would, in fact, have to conclude that Crane had considered but repudiated that argument.

Chapter VII is the first decisively interesting surviving example of Crane's revision of *The Red Badge*, and the revisions affect precisely this issue, shifting from explicit to implicit. This is the chapter in which Fleming is plunged from unworthy hope of personal justification into shame and self-pity by his deserted comrades' holding their line and repulsing the attack from which he had run. He seeks to "bury himself" in the thick woods, in nature. There he passes through swift changes of mood. "This landscape gave him assurance. A fair field holding life. It was the religion of peace. . . . He conceived Nature to be a woman with a deep aversion to tragedy." He shies a pine-cone at "a jovial squirrel" who dashes for safety: "The youth felt triumphant at this exhibition. There was the law, he said. Nature had given him a sign. . . . Nature was of his mind."

As he wends on, however, other signs obtrude. In a swamp he sees "a small animal pounce in and emerge directly with a gleaming fish." And finally, in what at first seems "a chapel" in a pine grove, he finds the disintegrating corpse of a Federal soldier from a bygone battle, with "black ants swarming greedily upon the grey face." The present text ends abruptly with Fleming fleeing the horror and leaving "the chapel" to the "soft wind" and "sad silence" of nature—[16] which ties in perfectly with an impressionistic bit of atmosphere about the onset of twilight which begins the next chapter.

Once, however, the text had been far more intellectually obvious, and Crane had kept it that way for quite a while. The "LV" manuscript, at least the third state, was revised first in pen, then in pencil. It was in that minimally fifth revision that Crane cancelled from the end of the chapter these words,

> Again the youth was in despair. Nature no longer condoled with him. There was nothing, then, after all, in that demonstration she gave—the frightened squirrel fleeing aloft from the missile. He thought . . . that there was given another law which far-over-topped it—all life existing upon death, eating ravenously, stuffing itself with the hopes of the dead. . . .[17]

That mood also passed. Shortly he is thinking as he heads back toward the battle that, because brambles restrain him, "Nature could not be quite ready to kill him."[18] But, of course, that alternation was lost from the revised text.

Fleming's nightmare agony in the middle part of *The Red Badge* climaxes in Chapter IX with the macabre death of Conklin, "the tall soldier," and in Chapter X with Fleming's desertion of "the tattered man" on being asked where his own wound was. Crane tried hard to provide Fleming with reflections adequate to his shocked and shame-sodden state but he failed, cancelling, rewriting, and cancelling again. He had Henry reflect, in utter opposition to his old romantic ideas, that soldiers were really "Nature's dupes." Nature went seducing men with "dreams" of "glory," defeating their ingenuity of devices to stave off death by planting a treacherous sentiment in their hearts. "War, he said bitterly to the sky, was a make-shift created because ordinary processes could not furnish deaths enough." From hints in "SV" Crane seems to have developed this and

Fleming's derisive fury about it for five pages in "LV."[19] He cancelled the effort out only in the blue-crayon revision of "LV" which appears to have gone to the typist.

That cancelled experience of Fleming's lay behind the returned motif of his exaltation of self-justification at seeing, at the beginning of Chapter XI, the routed troops on the road. That feeling is followed at once by his feeling like a sinner in Hell watching angels "with weapons of flame and banners of sunlight"[20] when a disciplined column of infantry butts its glorious way through the chaos. Crane stops to put Fleming through nine progressive states of psychosomatic and imaginary response to his situation in the least dramatic (and so perhaps least satisfactory) chapter in the book. And it was clearly Crane's intention in "SV" to follow the "analytic" chapter with a twelfth which would bring to an early climax both the theme of natural irresponsibility and the several times repeated theme of Fleming's prophetic role toward his comrades and the world.

Since the relative slackness of the previous chapter makes it clear that discursive patches mar *The Red Badge*, it is not surprising that Crane suppressed his intended Chapter XII. He was right to do so, and the principal use of considering it is to see that in it he unmistakably derided the naturalistic diagnosis of Fleming's condition together with Henry's Dreiser-like urge to proclaim its gospel. And he left (now submerged) that rejection as the pivot upon which Fleming could turn again, now fit to be delivered by kindly (but by no means unique, as it turned out) fates to his outfit.

That aborted chapter begins, "It was always clear to Fleming that he was entirely different from other men," and now he consoles himself that his suffering has been "unprecedented" in the awful opposition of his tiny self to the universe. But then he sees that there is no malice really, "merely law," and that there were compensating principles—what might be called the squirrel's law recurred to him:

> Nature had provided her creations with various defenses and ways to escape . . . that the things might resist or hide with a security proportionate to their strength and wisdom. It was all the same old philosophy. He could not omit a small grunt of satisfaction as he saw with what brilliancy he had reasoned it all out.

Soon he is ready to avail himself of that brilliancy and apply his findings to the incident of his own flight from the battle: "It was not a fault; it was a law. It was—But he saw that when he had made a vindicating structure of great principles, it was the calm toes of tradition that kicked it all down about his ears." In bitter rebellion he then resolves to save mankind from the worship of "the gods of the ashes," and he begins to see himself "the growing prophet of a world-reconstruction. Far down in the pure depths of his being . . . he saw born a voice. He conceived a new world, modelled by the pain of his life, in which no old shadows fell darkening upon the temple of thought. And there were many personal advantages in it."

He thinks of "piercing orations" and "himself a sun-lit figure upon a peak." But gradually his enthusiasm burns out as he thinks of mankind's bovine habitude—"he would be beating his fists against the brass of accepted things." He rails abuse "in supreme disgust and rage. . . . To him there was something terrible and awesome in these words spoken from his heart to his heart. He was very tragic."[21]

Crane's irony is obvious from the bathetic anti-climaxes of this: "And there were many personal advantages . . . a sun-lit figure. . . . He was very tragic." But even though this has disappeared from the text, its irony remains operative in the pivotal next chapter. There Fleming suddenly sees that all-enviable, heroic-angelic column charging back from the fray "like terrified buffaloes." He feels "horror-stricken" and stares "in agony and amazement." Then, most significantly, "He forgot that he was engaged in combating the universe. He threw aside his mental pamphlets on the philosophy of the retreated and rules for the guidance of the damned." He loses himself in concern for the stricken angels, thinks absurdly of rallying them, tries to detain one to ask what happened, and gets his red badge of courage from the rifle-butt in the hands of a hysterical ex-hero. His knockout is virtually a death, and for a while after he goes "tall soldier fashion." His first day of combat draws on to sunset, and in the dark he is rescued by the selfless and face-less "cheery soldier" and delivered back to the 304th New York where he belongs.

There he is met with cheer and sympathy. His lie about being shot readily believed, he is nursed and cared for by a suddenly mature, modest and no longer loud Wilson. In the morning he discovers that perhaps half the regiment had been missing after the action but turned up by morning with stories—"'Jest like you done,'" Wilson tells Fleming. Then, in a very late, blue-crayon cancellation surviving from two suppressed pages at the end of Chapter XIV ("LV"), he thinks "with deep contempt of all his grapplings and tuggings with fate and the universe." He sees how ridiculous had been the cherished uniqueness and novelty of his thought. But he begins to feel self-respect return-ing, since he is safe and "unimpeached."[22]

It will take all the rest of the last part of the book to try that egotism in the fire of a real, if minor, heroism and reduce it to the human modesty achieved by Wilson on the first day. From this point forward, however, nature will be no more abstracted, personified, or capitalized in *The Red Badge,* and Fleming's recollections of his prophetic ideas and role will be merely embarrassed. He will be glad nobody else knows. In-tellectually, that seems to be what there is to naturalism in the novel, and the symbolic or impressionistic uses of it are keyed to the intellectual.

It seems clear that *The Red Badge* is not a work of naturalism; and it is also certain that Fleming is *not* "guided by a naturalistic code of ethics." No more is a naturalistic "Henry's attitude . . . characteristic of Crane."[23] The true naturalist's truth must be that man is a part of nature and not other. Crane's sense of the in-difference or hostility of nature to man was shared, for instance, by a Pilgrim Father (Brewster), a Massachusetts Bay Puritan (Winthrop), a rationalistic Calvinist (Edwards), a deist (Freneau, "The Hurricane"), by Melville (whatever he was), and by many varieties of non-naturalistic Darwinists. Like them, Crane did believe man was "other"—in Crane's case, man was human. That was a lesson Henry Fleming learned to see.

IV

Then it becomes possible to say that *The Red Badge of Courage* is a work of psychological realism deeply affected in style by the fact that the author was also an ironic, imagistic, metaphysical poet. And that brings one to the moot questions of Crane's impressionism and symbolism. If one could be sure of the qualities of these, it would be best to treat them apart. Since, in fact, their existence as well as their separability is obscure, it may be best to take them together. Actually, in Crane's case it might be impossible to define his impressionism and symbolism separately.

"Impressionism" was a potent and intensely controversial term in the 1890's. A war cry for those who sought escape from Victorianism, it stood for the liberation of the artist from the academy and tradition, from formalism and ideality, from narrative, and finally even from realism; for realism demanded responsibility to the common vision and impressionism responsibility only to what the unique eye of the painter saw. It was also a swearword for conservatives of every variety, of course. In painting there was a solid body of reference, forged in the heat of often vicious controversy, and a body of distinguished (no matter how controversial) examples to give substance to "impressionism."

But in literature the case is and was different. The word was early applied to Crane's work. The *San Francisco Examiner* was working toward it from the hostile side when its paragrapher on January 12, 1897, objected to Crane and Garland together for "affectation in style," making "a dead set against literary rules [*sic*]" and to Crane separately for "the blare of his word-trumpets." And the *Chicago Record* got there the same week, observing on January 16 that "Mr. Crane is not a scientist. . . . He is above all an impressionist . . ."; "superficial," he was called, and also "flashy" in *The Little Regiment*; and the work was not up to "the fine psychological study" of *The Red Badge*.[24] On the other hand, it was repeatedly the highest praise of Joseph Conrad and Edward Garnett in England that Crane was an impressionist; it made him triumphantly avant garde. And that has given the word considerable currency in recent Crane criticism.

Nevertheless, it was and is difficult to know just what Crane's "impressionism" means. In literature the term is so vague and so devoid of explicit example as not even to make an entry in Wellek and Warren, *Theory of Literature*, or in standard histories. Handbook definitions, when they occur, are conspicuous neither for clarity nor richness of reference. They seem roughly agreed that in literature "impressionism" means either absence of detail

or else the effect of the author observing himself in the presence
of life, not the life.[25] Neither applies illuminatingly to the work
of Stephen Crane. Yet it would be strange if there were nothing
meant by all the often impressive critics who have applied the
term to Crane; and of course that is not the case.

What they are talking about comes down, perhaps, to the
vividness and intensity of Crane's notation of atmospheric
textures and to the striking economy, *multum in parvo,* of his
form. No doubt the effort to achieve psychological realism promoted what Willa Cather brilliantly defined as "The Novel
Démeublé."[26] Howells' first attempts at it in *The Shadow of a
Dream* (1890) and *An Imperative Duty* (1892) were strikingly
"disfurnished" after *A Hazard of New Fortunes* (1890). Crane's
own comment on literary aims is characteristically minimal and
apparently innocent of the term "impressionism" until his significant work had been done—and Conrad, Garnett, and others
had explained the avant garde situation to him. Even then he
carefully confined a striking use of it to painterly reference:

> The church had been turned into a hospital for Spanish
> wounded who had fallen into American hands. The interior of
> the church was too cave-like in its gloom for the eyes of the
> operating surgeons, so they had had the altar-table carried to
> the doorway, where there was a bright light. Framed then in
> the black archway was the altar-table with the figure of a man
> upon it. He was naked save for a breech-clout, and so close, so
> clear was the ecclesiastic suggestion that one's mind leaped to a
> fantasy that this thin, pale figure had just been torn down from
> a cross. The flash of the impression was like light, and for this
> instant it illumined all the dark recesses of one's remotest idea
> of sacrilege, ghastly and wanton. I bring this to you merely as
> an effect, an effect of mental light and shade, if you like; some-
> thing done in thought similar to that which the French im-
> pressionists do in color; something meaningless and at the same
> time overwhelming, crushing, monstrous.[27]

It has been persuasively argued that Crane must have learned
much and adapted to his writing what he learned of French
Impressionism.[28] Yet Linson, who should certainly have known,
denies it flatly—and apparently by implication denies the name
of "painter" to Vosburgh and the "Indians." Linson had been a
fellow student of Gauguin but not wholly in sympathy with

him. At least, however, Linson must be supposed to have known what Impressionism was all about:

> To the oft repeated query as to Crane's use of color: "Did he get it from his studio associates?" My answer is "No." I was the only painter among his early intimates; one or two others he met casually with me. The rest were illustrators or journalists. . . . The Impressionism of that day was to him an affectation, and all affectation was dishonesty, uncreative, and thus dead from the start.[29]

That statement can, of course, be regarded at most as authoritative only through Crane's establishment of himself in England.

Taken at fullest value, however, Linson indicates the same things shown by Crane's remark about Oscar Wilde: Wilde was "a mildewed chump." Crane was having none of the official *fin de siècle*. But he might equally well have had nonetheless his own sort of impressionism; and one can catch him at it. In "War Memories," again, there is a peculiar little moment when one almost feels embarrassed for Crane:

> "But to get the real thing!" cried Vernall, the war correspondent. "It seems impossible! It is because war is neither magnificent nor squalid; it is simply life, and an expression of life can always evade us. We can never tell life, one to another, although sometimes we think we can."[30]

Those Shelleyan cries and the slightly sissified self-consciousness about expression and the real thing are out of character for Crane. And, as a matter of fact, they constitute a strategic insincerity. He is embarking on a long series of pictures which will not "tell life" but present it unmistakably to a reader.

Actually Crane had, quite consciously, mastered the solution to that (as presented) pseudo-problem long before. In the *New York World* for October 15, 1896, for instance, he had lightened a bit of journalism for himself with a touch of virtuosity:

> We, as a new people, are likely to conclude that our mechanical perfection, our structural precision, is certain to destroy all quality of sentiment in our devices, and so we prefer to grope in the past when people are not supposed to have had any structural precision. As the terrible, the beautiful, the ghastly, pass continually

before our eyes we merely remark that they do not seem to be
correct in romantic detail.

But an odor of oiled woods, a keeper's tranquil, unemotional
voice, a broom stood in the corner near the door, a blue sky and
a bit of moving green tree at a window so small that it might
have been made by a canister shot—all these ordinary things
contribute with subtle meaning to the horror of this comfortable
chair, this commonplace bit of furniture that . . . waits and waits.

The subject is the electric chair at Sing Sing, and the virtuosity
is that he has solved the expressive problem in the act of describing it.

Not to choose any of the nature descriptions which set the
atmospheric stage so perfectly over and again in *The Red Badge*
or which tally Fleming's psychic gyrations, one bit of Crane's
special impressionism, his way of conveying the real thing with
extraordinary intensity, may stand for dozens. The 304th New
York has not quite gone into action when nearby "Saunders" gets
"crushed" by Confederates:

> The flag suddenly sank down as if dying. Its motion as it
> fell was a gesture of despair.
> Wild yells came from behind the walls of smoke. A sketch in
> gray and red dissolved into a mob-like body of men who galloped
> like wild horses.[31]

With minimal but exact detail, in an aura of psychological,
not objective, reality, the experience is precisely, forcefully
communicated. The method is more poetic than traditionally
novelistic, as has been variously observed. It is Crane's impressionism of texture. For the rest, the question has been most use-
fully approached through William M. Gibson's citation of the
letter from Thomas Wolfe to Scott Fitzgerald dividing great
writers into "putter-inners" and "taker-outers."[32] Crane belongs
with Flaubert, Hemingway, and Willa Cather's ideal as a "taker-
outer," and that trait perhaps is the other aspect of his impressionism.

Inescapably, when one considers Crane's abruptly vivid effects, the question arises whether they are just impressionistically
textural or symbolic as well. In some senses, of course, they are
immitigably symbolic, just as any word, any significant cluster

of words, is symbolic in any literary context. But surely that is not what is meant when Crane is called a "symbolist," for it would distinguish him not at all from any other author. In fact, to make the point one last time, it is hard to say what species, if any, of "symbolist" Crane was. No systematic discussion of that subject appears to exist. Certainly, as visionist, he represented the opposite of Charles Feidelson's "symbolistic imagination" and so he represents the opposite of Mallarmé, Baudelaire, *et seq.*[33] Crane was, that is, intensely concerned with the vision of realities, objective and subjective, which he regarded as independent of language but ideally susceptible of "unmistakable" communication through words. The evidence seems clear that he had no notion of any linguistically self-contained and unique literary "reality" and that he would have found that notion laughably conceited. One might, of course, argue, as exponents of some antirational schools of criticism appear to do, that, regardless of what Crane thought he thought, he was a "symbolist" because all good literature is such and so successful authors are this (or that) because their literature is good. But arguments of that sort are not available to discussion.

Thoroughly discussable, however, is what has become virtually a school of Crane criticism which follows the original ideas of the single most energetic, successful, and embattled of Crane scholar-critics, Robert W. Stallman. One can scarcely avoid concentrating discussion of the master, his disciples, and their doctrine on the problem of the most famous image in *The Red Badge of Courage*, now almost the best known image in American literature: "The red sun was pasted in the sky like a wafer."

Stallman's intuition that this is the central characterizing symbol of the whole work, from which the nature and stature of its artistry and the substance of its meaning must be interpreted, was promulgated in a forty-nine page introduction in the *Omnibus* (175-224). For Stallman the key to it all is that the "wafer" means the form of bread, circular, crisp, almost parchment-like, used in the celebration of the Eucharist in liturgical churches: "I do not think it can be doubted that Crane intended to suggest here the sacrificial death celebrated in communion." From this he argued back that Jim Conklin, the tall soldier who has died in the passages just preceding Crane's introduction of the image, is Christ, or a Christ-figure, and that the book then becomes, as Daniel Hoffman, accepting Stallman, says, "a chronicle of redemption."[34] The contention is that, as in Christian doctrine, Fleming is somehow redeemed by the sacrificial death of Conklin in a symbolic or "apocalyptic"[35] novel richly laden with Christian reference.

It should cause no wonder that such views have been not only doubted but challenged. A small critical war has been waged over them, with the balance appearing to turn of late against them.[36] The symbolist critics have obviously been useful in correcting overemphases on Crane's "naturalism," in stimulating study of his artistry, and in calling attention to achievements in that art which rise beyond what is usually subsumed under "impressionism." One thinks twice before rejecting the discoveries of well-informed, critically sensitive commentators. And it would be arrogant to deny that the childhood training and imaginative affinities of Stephen Crane should have led him to Christian imagery, or even perhaps to a pattern of Christian symbolism in *The Red Badge.* But, in all candor, many other critics simply cannot find such interpretations valid. The evidence adduced for the symbolic pattern breaks down at every point and at the first scrutiny. It is in fact not clear, first of all, that Crane as Crane is ever truly a symbolist: the test case may be "The Open Boat." Perhaps one needs to extend the sense of "impressionism" to take in what Crane does with images.

It would require a separate book to argue the problem out, but one can sketch the approaches to the problem by sticking to the wafer and Jim Conklin. To begin with, it was inherently improbable that Crane (whether he conceived the image *ab ovo* or read it in Kipling) thought of a "wafer" as eucharistic. He had been reared in an antiliturgical, enthusiastically anti-Catholic church and had become hotly anticlerical. While one could not rule out his knowing of the wafer of the Mass, he was much more likely to have thought of the word as denoting a confection or, as various critics have pointed out, an item of stationery common to and typical of the nineteenth century. As messy, expensive sealing wax passed out of use, it was replaced by a useful imitation of paper or other substance. Round, with neatly serrated edges stylizing the irregularities of a wax seal, often a deep, solid red as wax had been, these often gummed "wafers" were used to seal letters, packages, documents, etc. Joseph Her-

STEPHEN CRANE

gesheimer, reading Crane, "thought of an actual red wafer, such as druggists fixed to their bottles; it had a definite, a limited size for me, an established, clear vermilion color."[37]

Visualizing *that* kind of "wafer" expunges religious significance from the image, and it removes certain embarrassments, too. If the image were to be taken as seriously sacramental, why was it red? And if one strained toward a metaphysical answer to that, why, then, was it surrealistically "pasted"? Not to mention the most painful, there are embarrassments in the argument that the Lincolnesque Conklin is meant to represent Christ. As with the wafer, the connections seem hopelessly imprecise. Conklin does not bear the stigmata of Christ—even in his side. Christ's side was pierced after death by the spear of a professional soldier, iconography shows a neat, clean incision. Conklin's "side looked as if it had been chewed by wolves."[38] Nor will it do to argue that the sign is Fleming's recognition scream, "Gawd! Jim Conklin!" Thirteen lines later, Conklin is saying, ". . . Lord, what a circus! An' b' jiminey, I got shot. . . ."[39] Soldiers in *The Red Badge*, like real soldiers, frequently take the name of the Lord their God in vain—speaking not with symbolic portentousness any more than with blasphemous intent but simply as they speak (not in *The Red Badge*) obscenities for the registration of stereotyped and often comically inappropriate emotions.

The decisive difficulties with the Christian-symbolist reading of *The Red Badge*, it seems, are that there appears to be no way to make a coherent account of the symbols as referential to Christian doctrine and then to match that with what happens in the novel. The Christian doctrines of redemption and atonement, however central to orthodox faith, have ever been theologically obscure, intellectually mysterious. But they have always also been vital to Christian experience. And there just isn't any evidence of that, particularly as associated with the wafer and Conklin's death, in the after development of *The Red Badge*. There is textually no evidence that Fleming so much as perceives the "wafer." He mentions Conklin only once, informing Wilson of Jim's death, and they mourn briefly in the fashion of combat soldiers in the midst of death, ". . . poor cuss!"[40] Restored to self-esteem on his safe return to the regiment, Fleming quickly soars into an arrogance unpleasantly contrasted with Wilson's quiet manliness. At the end he has self-admiration to place beside humiliation as objects of contemplation. But it is his desertion of the live but dying tattered man which stabs his conscience. Conklin's death is absent from his thoughts.

It may be, in short, that Crane had no notion conscious or unconscious of "redemption" for Fleming. That may not have been his point at all, and the fact that one can gather a great deal of religious reference—or any other sort of reference—from the text may imply no hidden cohesions of meaning. Or it may: perhaps it is more a matter of whether one cares for Miss Caroline Spurgeon's methods with Shakespeare or not.

But in the end, the trouble with a "symbolic" reading of *The Red Badge* is that it assumes some sort of operative attitude toward a referential reality on the part of the artist. No matter how one qualifies it, a literary symbol must somehow be an image which points to something else, something usually conceptual. That "other" may be an established mythology accepted by artist and public; but nobody supposes that sort of integrative symbolism possible to Crane with Christianity. Or the artist may be in revolt, and the symbols disintegrative of the mythology—as dominantly in Melville. Or the symbols may refer to an arcane, even unique, mythology of the artist— in which case the interpreter must either be blanked or find the key to the arcanum.

The arcane way of a Blake or Yeats seems foreign to the temperament and known ideals of Crane. But it may be that symbolistic investigation of that possibility and of the disintegrative functions of Crane's religious imagery might prove more fruitful than those which have hitherto apparently assumed integrative patterns. Howells may well have been deeply perceptive in remarking that Crane had not yet got into the secret of himself. It might be possible to divine part of that secret by guessing at where Crane's religious insights were, perhaps unconsciously, leading him. On the other hand, humanistic and naturalistic interpreters have no doubt been right in seeing how the vision of *The Red Badge* scouted and reduced traditional religious as well as romantic securities. Perhaps such should pay more attention to the imagery as symbol.

In any case, symbolic or not, Crane's imagery has obviously

only begun to be comprehended. With a bewildering richness of reference (infraconceptual and so at first level imagistic and not symbolic), he wove a dense texture in *The Red Badge of Courage*. That, and not the often startling locutions, constitutes the triumph of its style. *The Red Badge* focuses only on three soldiers, Fleming and two who are obviously foils for him. One of them, Wilson, goes swiftly through the evolution from "loud soldier" to clear-sighted and therefore modest manhood which "The Veteran" testifies that Fleming also attained, perhaps by the end of the novel. But Wilson's transformation occurs while our eyes, which are Fleming's, are absent. Partly they are occupied with the death of "the spectral soldier," Jim Conklin.

If these common soldiers are representative as well as ordinary persons, Conklin is the representative sacrificed soldier, and he occupies in the novel a place equivalent to that of the Unknown Soldier in the national pantheon. His death deserves the emphasis its drama provides in *The Red Badge*. It is, as it must be, an occasion for shock and protest. Fleming incoherently registers it: "The youth turned, with sudden, livid rage, toward the battle field. He shook his fist. He seemed about to deliver a philippic. 'Hell—'" And nature, as it generally does in the novel, registers Fleming—the awful intensity but faceless frustration of the shock which cannot yet be grief: "The red sun was pasted in the sky like a wafer."

V

If style be taken as texture and form as structure, the question of the equal success of the novel's form depends on deciding the much-discussed problem of the ending. Does the novel end well? Does it end or just disappear? Is there a climax? Is the ending of the novel satisfactory, in short, in emphasis and substance?

Debate has raged since the early reviews, and much of it around the last chapter. Though many critics have not troubled to mention it, few would deny the real achievement of a climax in personal victory which comes at the end of the next to the last chapter. Jeered at by veterans, scorned by their general as "mud-diggers" and "mule drivers," barely surviving after a temporary desertion rate of nearly fifty percent on the first day, close to a "pretty success" which they had funked by a hundred feet a little earlier, the regiment had stood exasperatedly under a last pressure. Fleming, now a color-bearer, had resolved "that his final and absolute revenge was to be achieved by his dead body lying, torn and guttering, upon the field." His lieutenant had continued to curse, but it was now "with the air of a man who was using his last box of oaths."[41]

Then the men are ordered to charge and at last, tough, determined, sacrificial, soldier-like, they really do. Fleming forces the way, banner in hand, and Wilson captures the colors of the enemy. There arose "wild clamorings of cheers. The men gesticulated and bellowed in ecstasy." They had even taken prisoners. Fleming and Wilson sat "side by side and congratulated each other.", The narrative progression has been simple. Beginning in doubt about Fleming's—and the regiment's—courage, it had sunk to despair with his cowardice and Conklin's death. Now it rises to climax in their clear success, even, in a minimal sense, their heroism. The reversed curve is classic. And even more so is the reflective short downward curve of anticlimax at the end as the regiment is recalled and starts to wind its way back over the river and the men can suddenly realize that the battle is over.

As Fleming realizes this, his mind clears of "battle-sleep," and he is able to take stock. Crane trimmed quite a lot from the "LV" state of the last chapter, much of it reflecting too exactly the naturalistic debates he had earlier cut. But only one of the cuts was really important. What he was doing with Fleming, it seems clear, was not holding him up for judgment but rounding off the account of his experience. It was out of the question for Crane, insofar as he was a realist, to end a plot. It was neither with abstract structure nor with fable that he was concerned. The realists saw life as a continuum of the personal experiences of their characters. One broke in upon its flow at one significant point and left it at another. If in the course of this, one had any ulterior ideological motives, they should be planted out of sight and left for the reader to find.

As realist—psychological realist—as impressionist, perhaps even as metaphysician, Crane was, as we have seen, a visionist. The important thing was to see pellucidly and honestly. And what Crane is concerned with at the end of *The Red Badge* is what Fleming can see. By letting the readers see what Fleming sees,

Crane will let them decide what to think of him. Henry struggles "to marshal all his acts. . . . From this present point of view he was enabled to look upon them with some correctness, for his new condition had already defeated certain sympathies."

Supposing that the defeated sympathies are the multitude of earlier romanticisms, what does Fleming's cleared sight now reveal in those three ultimate pages of the novel? That his "public deeds" are glorious and impart a "thrill of joy" to his ego. But that he has incurred real shame, however hidden, for "his flight" and real guilt for the tattered soldier, "he, who blind with weariness and pain, had been deserted in the field." This vision and the fear of some impossible detection balance his self-glorification with "a wretched chill of sweat" and "a cry of sharp irritation and agony."

In the end he sees that he is neither a hero nor a villain, that he must assume the burdens of a mixed, embattled, impermanent, modest, yet prevailing humanity. He has discovered courage:

> . . . gradually he mustered force to put the sin at a distance. And at last his eyes seemed to open to some new ways. He found that he could look back upon the brass and bombast of his earlier gospels and see them truly. He was gleeful when he discovered that he now despised them.
>
> With this conviction came a store of assurance. He felt a quiet manhood, non-assertive but of sturdy and strong blood. He knew that he would no more quail before his guides, wherever they should point. He had been to touch the great death, and found that, after all, it was but the great death. He was a man.

If capturing the enemy flag climaxes the action of *The Red Badge*, this discovery of manliness concludes its exploration of ideas. The third major theme could not be concluded, however, since Fleming was not dead. It was the continuing notation of Fleming's psychological states which could only be harmonized in a sort of fade-out chord as Milton had done with the last lines of "Lycidas." Trying to force more out of these last sentences than Crane put there has caused unnecessary trouble for critics.

As he trudged away from "blood and wrath" Fleming's "soul changed"—as it had changed sometimes three times in a page earlier in the novel, though with more prospect of duration (not permanence) this time. Crane tried to end this three times before he got it right.[42] Finally he showed Fleming turning to a vision—"with a lover's thirst to images of tranquil skies, fresh meadows, cool brooks—an existence of soft and eternal peace." And a nature-image ends the book as one had begun it, the endlessly shifting nature registering the never settled psychological state in the last words. "Over the river a golden ray of sun came through the hosts of leaden rain clouds."

Was Henry Fleming then a hero? Well, yes—and no. It wasn't quite Crane's business to say so in *The Red Badge*, and he let it go to "The Veteran," which Eric Solomon very properly calls "A Gloss on *The Red Badge of Courage*."[43] There the reader sees that modesty, candor about his "flight," and a quiet courage to do what a man must do mark the veteran with the perspective of more battles and many years—as in two days they could never plausibly have marked "the youth." The ambiguities of Fleming's situation are natural. But Crane's irony bites only at his past delusions. He has become entitled to "images" of flowery peace.

The essence of that irony is that it would have been impossible for the early Fleming to judge whether the boy who had both "run" and borne the colors was hero or poltroon. He wouldn't, in fact, have known what he was talking about. He wouldn't have been able to see. From another point of view, Henry's heroism at its last is only common, the ordinary stock of courage among fighting men (or among truly living men and women), where what the visionless think "heroism" is as common as breathing. But from yet another point of view, the courage it takes to be human in the face of all the odds *is* magnificent, as only the extraordinarily sharp and realizing vision perceives. And it was Crane's sense of that in *The Red Badge*, as in much of the best of his work, which gives it an elevation and a pungency often tragic and always memorable. He talked about it overtly in "War Memories":

On the morning of July 2, I sat on San Juan Hill and watched Laughton's division come up. . . . There wasn't a high heroic face among them. They were all men intent on business. That was all. It may seem to you that I am trying to make everything a squalor. That would be wrong. I feel that things were often sublime. But they were *differently* sublime. They were not of our shallow and preposterous fictions. They stood out in a simple, majestic commonplace. It was the behavior of men on the street. It was the behavior of men. In one way, each man was just pegging along at the heels of the man before him, who was pegging along at the heels of still another man, who was pegging along at the heels of still another man who—It was that in the flat and obvious way. In another way it was pageantry, the pageantry of the accomplishment of naked duty. One cannot speak of it—the spectacle of the common man serenely doing his work, his appointed work. It is the one thing in the universe which makes one fling expression to the winds and be satisfied to simply feel.[44]

This passage was written at the end, when Crane was sick unto death and worn down to talking about it. In *The Red Badge of Courage* he was at a peak of his creative powers and could simply master the imaginations of readers with the power of an astonishing young genius presenting a masterpiece.

After *The Red Badge of Courage*

T HAT SENSE of the ambiguous sublimity of courageous
life in the face of the common fate, and the *Maggie* theme
of the tragic needs for pity and solidarity, became the centers
of all the rest of Crane's great work. Except for a few poems,
his future greatness was all to come out in the short story. The
one possible exception to that generalization would be *George's
Mother*. In length it is a *nouvelle*, as Henry James called the
form, at the most. But then, *The Red Badge* is hardly more;
and one apologizes, if apology is ever needed, for the lack of
complexity, of rich social involvement, which is the penalty
The Red Badge pays for its superb compression, by noting
that it too is perhaps a *nouvelle*. One does not expect of it what
Tom Jones or *The Portrait of a Lady* offer.

With *George's Mother* Crane returns to the slums to tell the
story of George's mother's losing fight to keep her boy uncor-
rupted in the Rum Alley neighborhood of *Maggie*. As she loses
George to drink, delinquency, and a sure future as a Bowery
bum, the mother loses her grip on life and slides away into death.
The accent falls on George's confusion of values between home,
mother, and church on one hand and street gang and saloon
on the other. A more careful and mature study than *Maggie*,
it lacks the dramatic intensity and compassion of Crane's first
slum book. Brief, cold, and disillusioned, it focuses as much on
George's cowardice as his bewilderment. It makes an interesting
forerunner, Protestant and Old New York in viewpoint, of James
T. Farrell's *Studs Lonigan*.

As this and all Crane's subsequent flights at the novel show, he
did not live to grow into the mastery of manners which might
have permitted the traditional novel, though he showed signs,

especially in "The Monster," of growing that way. There is no surprise, given the circumstances of his last five years (cf. Chapter II), in the fact that his three other efforts at the novel failed. The surprise lies in the greatness of the tales. It is, however, revealing to glance at these three attempts.

I

The Third Violet has by far the most charm. It came from a relatively happy and strong period of Crane's life, written in the midst of his perturbations over the success of *The Red Badge* and done because he wanted to do it—with some misgivings but *con amore*. It attempted to make use of Crane's experiences with painters and "Indians," and its hero, Hawker, was apparently more or less modeled on Linson. Crane had disclosed glimmers of capacity to dramatize manners in moments of *Maggie* and in incidental writings like "Mr. Binks' Day Off" and "An Experiment in Luxury." There is no doubt that maturity and adult experience would have ripened his powers to true mastery of the great tradition in the novel. But *The Third Violet* tends to show why novelists are seldom great before the age of forty. By contrast, it shows how youthful yet unique, how experimental yet inherently brilliant, Crane's best writing is.

The Third Violet, though exploiting autobiography, was a fascinating attempt to imitate William Dean Howells. The first part takes place in a resort like Hartwood, where Hawker has returned to his farm home to paint and where he sees and falls in love with Miss Fanhall at the summer hotel and courts her on the tennis court, on picnics, walks, etc., with the help of his friend Hollanden, a cool Craneian writer. Howells, of course, had virtually invented the summer-vacation novel, had turned it into a *genre* convertible for all sorts of purposes, and had made its exploitation a steady part of his career. The other half of Crane's book was placed among the "Indians" of the Art Students' League Building. Howells, beginning with *A Hazard of New Fortunes*, was devoting much of his output in the 1890's to the problems of the artist in New York. *The World of Chance* had barely ceased publication in *Harper's Monthly* for November, 1892, when *The Coast of Bohemia* (which dealt in part with the students of the League before they moved out of their old

Building) began to run in Bok's *The Ladies' Home Journal* for December.

Crane of course knew and could do things Howells couldn't. Widely acquainted with painters, sculptors, architects of his own day, Howells knew Crane's generation best through his son, John Mead, and his daughter, Mildred. The impecunious "Comanches" of *The Third Violet*, fine portraits, and the model, Florinda "Splutter" O'Connor, a Maggie competent for survival, were as beyond Howells as the wonderful sketches of "Stanley"— a "large, orange and white setter." There are many fine touches in *The Third Violet* to prove that it was written by Stephen Crane: Hawker's perceptively studied farm folks; the Hartwood scenery; the Bohemians at home—"Wrinkle," "Great Grief" Warwickson, "Penny" Pennoyer, "Purple" Sanderson; and of course Splutter and Stanley. These characters are all minor, however. It was in the perceptions of the real situations of the major characters and in the clarification of ideas to which those perceptions should have led that Crane fell down.

Probably it did not occur to Crane that Howells had spent thirty years learning how. Of course Howells, disillusioned of egalitarian myth, had discovered the broad drama involved in a situation like Crane's confrontation of poor, farmerish, gifted, artistic, personally superior Hawker with rich, urban, cultivated, sensitive but snobbish Miss Fanhall. It confronted two basic, fascinating American types, as Howells saw early: the "Social" and the common, the "conventional" and "unconventional," Society's lady and nature's gentleman. Over many years, with deepening perception and disillusion, Howells had studied the implications of all this until it had made an independent, semi-religious, and democratic socialist of him. In *The Third Violet* Crane saw only personal injustice and amatory affront. Similarly, Crane wholly failed to dramatize the point Howells was making about the artist in a world of chance: that the combat conditions of a competitive, acquisitive society stifled art. Having the Bohemians just talk about it was not enough.

It was, however, only immaturity, not seeing far enough, which held Crane back. Intrinsically, the situation he had imagined was far more immediate and dramatic in its potential, far more modern, than any comparable situation in Howells. After having Hawker woo Miss Fanhall in an inconclusive idyll, Crane transports him back to the city and a triangle. "Splutter" O'Connor, a "very honest" Irish girl with "a beautiful figure" frankly carries a torch for Hawker. Crane develops the setting, the *dramatis personae*, and the conflict in class, character, candor, and personal reality (much in "Splutter's" favor) between the two women—and then abruptly deserts it for a foggy final scene in which Miss Fanhall starts to brush Hawker off, as Hawker had done to "Splutter," and then incomprehensibly reverses herself and accepts him.

The failure to face and develop the conflicts of class and convention, of sex and of art against society, destroys the novel and strips its deficiencies of all concealment. Its fragmentary brevity, its lack of competence to carry off scenes requiring the full development of conversation, its confusion of ideas and missed opportunities of a dozen sorts, and its ultimate lack of achieved, over-all form protrude like the skeleton of a half-built house. And the key to all this failure is easily seen on consideration to be Crane's entire inability to comprehend women, especially Miss Fanhall.

It was not necessary to her case that Crane should understand Maggie Johnson personally, or even consider viewing her from within. Not explaining her either, he does a good introductory job of communicating the personality of "Splutter" O'Connor. But, as Carl Van Doren said of the women of *Active Service*, "with young girls [Crane] never outgrew the young man's sense that they are cryptic creatures, whose words never mean what they seem to say and whose silences are deeply mysterious." They are "incomprehensible."[1] That is everywhere true, but triply so if they are ladies. Crane's ladies are just about what Lowell said of Fenimore Cooper's, "Sappy as maples and flat as his prairies."

That sappiness had some warrant in Howells, who had made a life-long study and some wonderful comedy of the vagaries of feminine logic, of the irresponsible emotionalities, and of the quixotisms of ladies full of a dangerous pride in the little knowledge they had gleaned from romances. Howells had not in several instances been above the trick, once his real story was told, of sugar-coating it for the hopeless magazine reader with a story-rounding "happy" ending based on such illogic—

secure in the faith that perceptive readers would enjoy the joke and others would never feel the irony till they sneezed.

The real trouble with *The Third Violet* and *Active Service* is that, in dealing with women in fiction, Crane's irony deserted him. He did not have a clear single view of them, much less a double or triple vision. One of the difficulties, in fact, of accepting the recurrently popular notion that Crane's early "affairs" were more than the passion of the moth for the star, that he was a roistering whore-chaser, an experienced lover before Cora, a trapped exemplar of Freud's case of "A Special Type of Choice of Object Made by Men,"[2] is that none of this experience did anything for his imagination. If such experience existed, it was, among Crane's experiences, uniquely unavailable to his creative mind. The sole exception, which is post-Cora, is the troubled poem "Intrigue."

Except for the almost laughably romantic portrait of Nora Black, *femme fatale* and war correspondent like Cora, and who was probably derived from Cora, Crane's women are imagined exactly as they might have been had he been quite innocent, quite normal. Perhaps he was. Marjory Wainwright of *Active Service* is portrayed no more sophisticatedly than Miss Fanhall. And Nora Black, as Carl Van Doren said, is handled "with a boy's ferocity. Snubs which would batter an ordinary woman into pulp only accelerate her pursuit of the cool hero. She is no less a myth than eager Venus on the trail of young Adonis."[3]

For the rest, it seems impossible to improve on Van Doren's criticism of *Active Service* as far as it goes. Beyond Van Doren, the significance of *Active Service* and Crane's first twenty-five percent of *The O'Ruddy* lies in their revelation of the late, desperate, and pathetic struggle of Crane's integrity with best-sellerism. In the age of *Trilby, Graustark,* and *When Knighthood Was in Flower,* inferior literary talents coined money in such golden floods as had never before been won by authors. Cuban glory, an exasperated consciousness that his superior talent still earned far too little, haste, and that pressure of money for "Brede" which Ford and Liebling believed killed Crane, all tempted him to cash in on the fad. In pieces like "The Private's Story" and "The Clan of No-Name" he gave in occasionally to embarrassingly Kiplingesque ideas and mannerisms.

But his surrender was never for long. It seems that he wrote *Active Service* at all only because Harold Frederic insisted he must: it would be the salvation of his career. Frederic knew how to grind them out; Cora must hold Stephen to it. But if neo-romanticism were to be his salvation, Crane was not to be saved. He could not resist the realist's game of blowing it up and then puncturing it. In *Active Service* he sends Coleman, the correspondent, to rescue Marjory Wainwright at the front. Coleman loves "reflecting upon the odd things which happen to chivalry in the modern age . . . he made no effort to conceal from himself that the whole thing was romantic" but took "a solemn and knightly joy in this adventure." As Crane builds it up, Coleman sees himself "dealing with a medieval situation with some show of proper form: that is to say, armed, a-horseback, and in danger, then he could feel that to the Gods of the game he was not laughable." He "took satisfaction in his sentimental journey. It was a shining affair. He was on active service, an active service of the heart . . . even as the olden heroes . . . he had never known that he could be so pleased with that kind of parallel."

Coleman prospers as Minniver Cheevy, however, no better than Henry Fleming had. At the first real danger he is lost: "He would not have denied that he was squirming on his belly like a worm through black mud," and yearning to get out. "If his juvenile and uplifting thoughts of other days had reproached him he would simply have repeated and repeated: 'Adventure be damned.' "[4]

The same feelings motivated the design for, and the first quarter Crane lived to write of, *The O'Ruddy*. Crane's historical imagination was keen, but he never had confused things either by supposing that he could seriously re-enter the past or by lacking respect for the sense of the past because it was imaginary. Therefore to him the irresponsible historical romance was fair game. In *The O'Ruddy* he tried to write a sword-clashing, picaresque, true-love-laden, coincidence-packed romance *and* make fun of the silly, golden *genre* by burlesquing it with the best sustained humor he had yet achieved. All the life goes out of style and characterization when Robert Barr, or whoever it was, takes over.[5] Barr's troubles were not, as he supposed, with plot so much as with focus of character, tone, atmosphere, and dialogue. If Crane had lived, *The O'Ruddy* might have been a brilliant *tour de force* on themes by the ghostly Stevenson.

II

After *The Red Badge*, then, Crane's aspiring novels are about what one would expect of a novelist his age: essentially auto-biographical, occasionally intense, sporadically gifted, weak in characterization, fragmentary in form. A number of the short stories, on the other hand, are absolutely first-class; some of them are of definitive, classic stature. It is a measure of the great-ness of the best that there can be space to discuss only those few and that the others, so very good, must be let go.

Widely anthologized as a standard representative of the short story and Crane's work, "The Open Boat" has too often been appreciated for biographical or tendentious reasons and too seldom for its authentic artistic power. The tale has re-peatedly been called naturalistic, even the one pure American example of naturalism; or impressionistic; or the work of a symbolist, or even of an existentialist.[6] And commentators have been peculiarly tempted to the exercise of the biographic fallacy—the identification of the author himself with the interior substance of the fiction—by the circumstances of the story's provenience. As we have seen, Crane *was* shipwrecked, spent long hours at sea in a dinghy, was swamped in the surf, and lost Billy Higgins coming ashore. He did write up all but the dinghy voyage for the *New York Press,* and wise anthologists have of late found it useful to print the account *seriatim* with the fiction. Crane (or Scribner's) did subtitle it: "A Tale Intended to be after the Fact. . . ."

"After the Fact" here may as well be in pursuit of the truth of experience as of the mere exact occurrence, however—and in Crane it is much more likely to be. Actually, "The Open Boat" seems one case in which a grasp of the methods of Crane the visionist, the perspectivist, reconciles all difficulties. As most modern critics have seen, and as most undergraduates recognize on comparing the news report and the story, the latter is al-together a work of art. That being true, the biographical events were at best the occasions for the tale; it does not in the least matter that Crane may have made free imaginatively with the wind, weather, or anything else; and to identify Crane himself with "the correspondent" in the fiction is naïve.

The very essence of Crane's art and achievement in "The Open Boat" is his control—subtle, complex, and intense—of its internal points of view. The famous opening line announces the centrality of point of view: "None of them knew the color of the sky." Why not? Their group point of view was concentrated on the never-ending athletic feat of surmounting each gray, snarling, "barbarously abrupt and tall" wave which tried to capsize their dinghy and drown them. That group viewpoint, uniting the men in a brotherhood of danger, is the first, least usual, and most important of three points of view in the story. The other two are that of the neutrally observing narrator, who reports dramatically on the scenes which occur among the men, and that of the intellectual in the boat, the correspondent. It matters immensely to an understanding of the story that one see through which point of view events are conveyed.

Crane's newspaper account has the fact-perspective of his journalism: strong in effects yet told in a flat, technically "objective," first-person narrator's voice. The significant thing about the fiction is that the major perspectives are those of the characters. They know the human solidarity and the generosity (best shown by Billy the oiler) of men whose eyes are cleared to see that they face death. One of them has shifting fantasies, certainly psychological and perhaps symbolic, as he rows through the darkness. At the end, with Billy in his grave and themselves safely abed—"When it came night, the white waves paced to and fro in the moonlight, and the wind brought the sound of the great sea's voice to the men on the shore, and they felt that they could then be interpreters."

It may be that the real implications of Cyrus Day's challenging reconstruction of the nice day on which the *Commodore* sank, and of the ethical problems of Captain Murphy, are that "the facts," the actualities of his open-boat experience were so ambiguously bathetic that Crane made no attempt to transcribe them. He set to work to imagine it as a trope of man's condition face to face with nature, fate, and death. At any rate, the story certainly is such a trope. This being true, the polarity of points of view in the story is all important. If Stephen Crane can ever be unmistakably shown to be a symbolic naturalist, it is in "The Open Boat." But to prove him so is to exercise the biographic fallacy and identify him with the correspondent and his thoughts with the correspondent's thoughts. For it is in the correspondent's mind and point of view that the key symbolic perceptions occur in the story.

Rowing all alone in the darkness with the others plunged in exhausted sleep, the correspondent begins to think in Section VI of the story: "If I am going to be drowned . . . why . . . was I allowed to come thus far and contemplate sand and trees?" The voice which succeeds is that of the summarizing neutral narrator. But what he summarizes is so placed in the framework of the correspondent's reveries that it is unmistakably the substance of the correspondent's thought. He thinks that to drown him would be "an abominable injustice" and a "crime most unnatural" to a man "who had worked so hard, so hard." And then it occurs to him that "other people had drowned at sea since galleys swarmed with painted sails," and he is led to reflect despairingly on the quality of what is natural and where man stands:

> When it occurs to a man that nature does not regard him as important, and that she feels she would not maim the universe by disposing of him, he at first wishes to throw bricks at the temple, and he hates deeply the fact that there are no bricks and no temples. Any visible expression of nature would surely be pelleted with his jeers.
> Then, if there be no tangible thing to hoot, he feels, perhaps, the desire to confront a personification and indulge in pleas, bowed to one knee, and with hands supplicant, saying, "Yes, but I love myself."
> A high cold star on a winter's night is the word he feels that she says to him. Thereafter he knows the pathos of his situation.

This reflection is, of course, not unrelated to the collective point of view of the men in the boat. They had earlier, upon not quite daring to try the surf on the beach, rejected the idea that the "old ninny-woman, Fate," might dare to drown them. And the narrator comments that this present content of the correspondent's thought, while discussed by nobody, had no doubt been reflected upon by each man "in silence and according to his mind." It is nowhere suggested, however, that the correspondent's conclusions are those of the group. On the contrary, when in the morning they head for the beach again and see the white windmill, Crane explicitly gives it to the correspondent to see it symbolically: "It represented in a degree, to the correspondent, the serenity of nature amid the struggles of the individual—nature in the wind, and nature in the vision of men. She did not seem cruel to him then, nor beneficent, nor treacherous, nor wise. But she was indifferent, flatly indifferent."

"The Open Boat" gains its greatest force, then, from a metaphysical tension between two opposing possibilities of the meaning of the death of Billy the oiler, as these possibilities are registered in the two kinds of character perspective. In the correspondent's point of view naturalism is almost classically presented. Nature is flatly indifferent, man will lose his struggle to survive; nature is therefore implicitly contemptuous and hostile; and man is absurd and the proper object of self- (since none else can feel it) pity. This gives rise to the naturalistic tragedy of pathos and bathos.

The opposing possibility, implicit in the heroism, the generosity, and the death in victory of Billy, implies of course a wholly opposite set of conclusions. The most admirable man in the boat, whose life is laid down for his friends, Billy is certainly no less a Christ-figure than Melville's Billy Budd. His function in the story seems much more obviously Christ-like than Jim Conklin's in *The Red Badge*. He plays the greatest part in creating the human solidarity, the brotherhood, the capacity for real pity, the disinterested "love of Being in general" which makes man in the story anything but absurd. Billy dies, but he gets his comrades safe to shore. The implication is that man by courage and complicity can rise superior to the pathos of his situation; he can understand it and answer it with the magnificence of his defiance, his acceptance, and perhaps even his use of it to achieve a classically tragic elevation.

The tension between these two polar possibilities is left unresolved in "The Open Boat." For readers, certainly the complexities raised by that tension make for experience of a far higher order than the merely naturalistic, as may be seen by comparing its effects with those of the ending of Hemingway's *A Farewell to Arms*. That remains true even if one ends by declaring for the naturalistic interpretation. I think, however, that Crane, in this one of the greatest of his short stories, meant the same sort of ambiguity to stand as that which we find in the greatest of Hawthorne's short stories. Tension stands, and courage and negative capability are essential until one finds, as Crane never did, a way to resolve it.

III

The second of Crane's unmistakably great short stories, "The Blue Hotel," has also stirred up a vortex of warring criticism.[7] Though some of the symbol-hunting has ranged past the point of the ludicrous, that criticism has not left much of the story unexplored. The comments of Joseph Satterwhite and Stanley B. Greenfield are particularly helpful. In much of the criticism the most striking feature is the resolute explaining away of portions of the text in order to make the story conform with the critics' predetermination that it shall be a work of naturalism. Actually, however, "The Blue Hotel" is no more purely naturalistic than any of Crane's other major work.

It tells the story of the irruption upon the sleepy little town of Fort Romper, Nebraska, of a hysterical foreigner, a Swede, who turns up at Scully's Palace Hotel in the midst of such a raging blizzard as Crane had seen scourging the farmers on his Western tour. Moody and jittery, announcing that he knows he will be killed, the Swede challenges the hospitable instincts of the hotelkeeper. Scully bucks him up with liquor and good fellowship, whereupon his guest turns insufferably arrogant. There is an uneasy card game which leads to a fist-fight between the Swede and Scully's son. Victorious and more arrogant than ever, the Swede checks out of the hotel, swaggers down the street to a saloon, tries to force the local gambler to drink with him, makes the mistake of manhandling the gambler, and is stabbed to death. In a final scene two of the other erstwhile guests of the blue hotel, the cowboy and the Easterner, talk the tragedy over.

There is no evidence in the story that it is nature or any other deterministic force which kills the Swede. No "force" compelled him to come to Fort Romper, and certainly none compelled him to mistake it for the Wild West. The cowboy's exasperated objections to the delusive quality of the Swede's perceptions are well taken. But it is apparently Crane's *donnée* that a lifetime of dime-novel romanticism about the West shall be a condition of the Swede's neurosis. Crane neither asserts nor denies that such romanticism may in itself have unhinged the Swede. He merely gives us an unhinged foreigner mad with the conviction of his impending death, his compulsion to find it, and a fixation upon violence which is properly only fictional. As we should now say, the Swede is a perfect example of the self-fulfilling prophecy.

One of the most intriguing factors in the story is the blueness, the shrieking, outrageous saturation of the color of Scully's Palace Hotel. What does that represent? A really satisfactory answer might provide one a key to all Crane's famous use of color and color words. But one of the most interesting things about all the criticism is that nobody appears to have found the key either to the general question or to the specific case. This suggests that perhaps there is no key. Perhaps Crane found color significance where he found it, pluralistically, on an *ad hoc* basis, without a generalizable or theoretical ground for what he did.

Most obviously, the hotel's business is commercial. Nobody passes the town on the train or enters the town from the train without seeing, remembering, and perhaps entering the blue hotel. Beyond that, one can read all sorts of significances into the defiance of that color. It may be man's "coxcombry" against the blizzard of the universe, that conceit which is "the very engine of life." It may be for old Scully, the one quite human being in the story, the assertion of his humanness. On the other hand, it may be the Swede's rejection of humanity for that frantic, romantic dream which brings him the "purchase" of his death, or it may be the failure of the other men to join Scully's effort to treat the Swede as a man and brother which makes them complicitly guilty of his death.

For some readers, the story has seemed properly to end at the conclusion of Section VIII, where, "The corpse of the Swede, alone in the saloon, had its eyes fixed upon a dreadful legend that dwelt atop of the cash-machine: 'This registers the amount of your purchase.'" The final section, IX, has been a scandal and a stumbling block to no few commentators partly because it challenges a simply naturalistic reading of the story, partly because it quite explicitly introduces moral ideas and militates against the notion that Crane is always a non-ideological symbolist in his art. Actually, what the addition of that final page-and-a-half does to the story is greatly to enrich it by deliberately reversing its moral perspectives and restoring them to the same challenging ambiguity between naturalistic and at least humanistic perspectives of "The Open Boat."

When the silent little Easterner suddenly breaks silence to explain the situation to the cowboy, naturalistic symbols, atmospheres, and ironies are totally missing. The language, the irony, and the symbolic drama are now moralistic; the sanctions behind them are humanistic if not religious. As a matter of fact, the perspective of the Easterner is that of Christianity as interpreted by Tolstoi and no doubt mediated to Crane through Howells. This is the language, just as it is the strategy of presentation, of that doctrine of complicity which Howells had been developing in book after book during the ten years before Crane left New York for Cuba. "We are all in it!" says the Easterner, ". . . every sin is the result of a collaboration. We, five of us, have collaborated in the murder of this Swede. Usually there are from a dozen to forty women really involved in every murder, but in this case it seems to be only five men—you, I, Johnnie, old Scully; and that fool of an unfortunate gambler came merely as a culmination, the apex of a human movement, and gets all the punishment." And the cowboy, to point up the irony, is given the line behind which every one would like to hide from the searching finger of his complicit guilt in the world: "Well, I didn't do anythin', did I?"

If one reflects back—as Crane clearly intended one should —from this point across the whole of the preceding story, he sees that this is not an appendage upon the tale: it provides another point of view. Though it has not been popular to do so, one might have read the story of the Swede as one does the stories of so many of the characters of Stephen Crane's great contemporary, Edwin Arlington Robinson. Perhaps the Swede was a kind of combination of Minniver Cheevy and Richard Cory. Or, of course, as it has been most popular to show, the Swede's story might be one of symbolic naturalism. The final section of "The Blue Hotel" provides a third perspective, one without which the story is far less significant than the great work Crane gave us. It seems hardly necessary to detail all the implications of that multiplicity. No criticism of the story, however, can finally be taken seriously which confines itself to less than the full complexity of its perspectives.

IV

"The Open Boat" and "The Blue Hotel" are the sort of intense stories of masculine adventure, action, tragedy, and irony which it is generally agreed that Stephen Crane did supremely well. There has been too little tendency to grant him also the power to deal with the homely, domestic, and commonplace tragedies of society and the ironic examinations of manners which have characterized American realism at its most typical and best. It was toward this which he must have grown had he matured into an achieved mastery of the novel in its traditional forms and concerns. It was this toward which he must have matured if he were to have matched Robinson or Joyce in his own way. But there has been too easy an assumption that, because the financially desperate and physically dying Crane of his last eighteen months obviously declined in creative power, his genius had actually preceded his body in death, his talent been burned out.

In the premises, of course, no such assumption is necessary. And actually Crane showed in some of the later writings great promise of proceeding toward the perceptions and problems necessary to his maturing. Such development may be seen in "The Monster," in "The Bride Comes to Yellow Sky," and in the best of the *Whilomville Stories*. In these for the first time in Crane one is moving toward a dense, adult, demonstratedly complicit society. The great vein of the major novelists, the novel of manners, is beginning to open. Crane's is a world not only of young men and children but of grown men and of grown, non-chivalric, and comprehensible women. It is not surprising that Crane turned to the exploitation of the *genre* of the boy book which had been developed by the American realists. But it was less to be expected that he should now take up the theme which Twain and Howells had prepared for Crane's generation—especially Cather, Anderson, and Masters—the theme best labeled by Sinclair Lewis's original title for *Main Street*, "The Village Virus." In Whilomville and in Yellow Sky the terror and the beauty of the American small town's security and boredom and vulnerability are as beautifully portrayed as they would be by any of the specialists to come of that theme.

If he did not temperamentally suspect it before he went, Stephen Crane spotted the secret of the romantic West the moment he got there. And he told it delightfully in "The Bride Comes to Yellow Sky." The secret which Roosevelt, Wister, and Remington would not let themselves believe was not only that the Wild West of romance did not exist but that it never had. Natty Bumppo and all his descendants had been *beaux idéals,* privileges of the romancer. Romance was always somewhere, sometime else. "This ain't Wyoming, ner none of them places," says a "deeply scandalized" cowboy in "The Blue Hotel," "This is Nebrasker." The best the frontier could offer were the raw, hoodlum tests of courage of "A Man and Some Others" or "Horses —One Dash." Courage was always splendid—but what tested it might be evil, stupid, or merely absurd. The reality of the West, of the frontier, is the exoreism of chimeras like Scratchy Wilson by the mere advance of social realities like the marriage of the marshal to a commonplace little waitress from San Anton'. The proper mode of dealing with the theme was comic, that of social comedy, and Crane hit it perfectly in his story.

The same sense of social reality dominates the non-mythic stories of initiation which Crane told of the boys in Whilomville. The best of these—"The Stove," "The Knife," or "His New Mittens"—throw a good deal of light on "The Monster," the major work Crane imagined from the same setting. Here Crane begins with what at first looks like a fairly ordinary Stephen Crane concern for the nature, conditions, quality, and fate of heroism. But he proceeds within a uniquely dense web of multiple characters and of social reference. The compact descriptions of the substance and quality of the life of the village in its many social levels are brilliantly effective. The accuracy of Crane's sense of all sorts and conditions of men, women, and children is unexpected in the author of the almost abstracted characters of *Maggie* and *The Red Badge*. Crane never lets go of this exploration in a new, social context of his themes of courage and heroism; but, by the time one is half way through the story, he has become aware that the title is as essential and as pregnant as that of a poem by George Herbert.

Briefly, the story is that of Dr. Trescott, whose Negro stableman is horribly burned, mutilated, and reduced to idiocy in rescuing Trescott's son from a fire. Whilomville's first reaction to this, when it thinks Henry Johnson is going to die, is a sensational, romantic exaltation of his heroism. Trescott labors, with his own heroic devotion, to save Henry's life. But he cannot save his mind or his face. Gradually the sentiment of the town swings to revulsion against the poor derelict. Trescott, however, will neither forget nor cancel his debt of admiration and gratitude. Hysteria mounts. By the end of the tale, Trescott is suffering professional boycott and social ostracism for sheltering a monster.

The question becomes, Who is the Monster? And by the time one is done pondering all the elements and implications of scene and action, he comes to a chilling conclusion. Everybody is. This is true in some sense for every individual character, at every social level, in the village. And it is true for the village as a whole. In fact, by the end it is the village itself, especially in its most respectable and dominant society, which is most particularly the monster. Crane has never had to editorialize, but the indictment is colder, more furiously returned than in any comparable work. "The Monster" cries out for a more adequate criticism than it has received.[8]

V

Like pluralistic views of Crane's approaches to life and literature, appreciation of this latter development of his imagination spoils the harmony of any simple, unitary view of what he was and could do. It also challenges the notion of a burned out Crane whose death was no real loss to American letters. On the contrary, one remains convinced that the loss of Stephen Crane was a real tragedy to the development of our literature, our culture. Mr. A. J. Liebling has put it well: "I think, myself, that Crane might have written long novels of an originality as hard to imagine, in retrospect, as *Maggie* and *The Red Badge* would have been to anticipate."[9] Crane's death and then that of Frank

Norris left his generation of novelists reduced essentially to Theodore Dreiser. Whatever one thinks of Dreiser's genius, it is clear that it could have profited immensely from the context of real contemporaries as gifted as Norris and Crane. And I, for one, think that Crane's gifts ranged widely beyond and above those of Dreiser. The tragedy of Crane's early silencing, quite apart from any element in it personal to Crane, is that of the death of any gifted young person. It is the tragedy of the unperformed, the unrealized, the never to be known.

In the end the real power of Stephen Crane is in awareness, the power to register and to make the reader see what he saw. Regardless of qualifiers, of what the vision saw, he is supremely a visionist. The one greatest unfairness dealt him has been the repeated implication that it was romantically himself he was trying to make the reader see. On the contrary, the essence of his art was to give, in his characters, persons with eyes and to set them in turn within perspectives which would let readers see both very sharply and complexly around them and so to feel life as Crane felt it. That is true of every great artist. It is equally true of them all that, having felt their power, one must decide for himself how far to accept it. Crane's vision was preternaturally "modern" in its progression to irony. Accept it or not, no honestly hospitable reader can deny either the power of its artistic transmission or, therefore, the youthful yet permanent greatness of Stephen Crane.

Notes and References

References to items listed in the Selected Bibliography are identified by author and by list-number in the bibliographies: e.g., "Colvert, No. 14."

Introduction

1. "Stephen Crane: Lost and Found," *Saturday Review of Literature*, XXXIV (February 3, 1951), 21ff.

Chapter One

1. It is precisely the point here, of course, that this is an association often, almost naturally, made. It was recognized explicitly in Crane's own time (see "Stephen Crane: 'A Wonderful Boy,'" *Literary Digest*, June 23, 1900) and later by Amy Lowell, Vincent Starrett, and Alfred Kazin among many others.

Whatever its limitations, there is now a broadly accepted tradition of Crane biography. It might be described as the area held largely in common by the six "basic" Crane books, plus a number of biographically significant articles, and such works as Cady and Wells, No. 11; Colvert, No. 14; Franchere, No. 26; O'Donnell, No. 44; Schoberlin, No. 51; Stallman, No. 55; and Zara, No. 64. In the first two biographical chapters of this book, material generally derivable from this tradition has not been cited to any single source. Special and particular debts have been acknowledged.

2. R. W. Stallman and Lillian Gilkes, eds. *Stephen Crane: Letters*, [hereafter *Letters*], p. 119.

3. "Stevie," *New York Evening Literary Review*, July 12, 1924.

4. Cady, No. 11, p. 11.

5. "The Merry Throng at Hot Springs," Philadelphia *Press*, March 3, 1895.

6. L. U. Pratt, "The Formal Education of Stephen Crane," *American Literature*, X (January 1939), 461.

7. Cady, No. 11, pp. 2-4.

8. "The Merry Throng at Hot Springs."

9. Chas. Michelson, *The Work of Stephen Crane*, 1925-1926 [hereafter called *Work*], Vol. XII, pp. xii-xiii, xvii-xix.

10. *Letters,* p. 319.

11. John D. Barry, editor of *Forum,* thought so; and Barry was apparently more actively impressed by Crane's "lines" than anyone else at the moment.

12. The terribly difficult business of dating both this and *The Red Badge* has been clarified by Pizer, No. 47.

13. See Corwin K. Linson, *My Stephen Crane,* ed. by E. H. Cady, 1958 [hereafter "Linson"], p. 86; *Letters,* pp. 56, 58.

14. See especially T. F. O'Donnell, "Notes on the Reception of Crane's *The Black Riders,*" *American Literature,* XXIV (May 1952), 233-34.

15. *Letters,* p. 73.

16. Cady, No. 11, pp. 29, 68.

Chapter Two

1. Cady, No. 11, p. 42.

2. *Letters,* p. 106.

3. *Ibid.,* p. 107.

4. Cf. Floyd Dell, "Stephen Crane and the Genius Myth," *Nation,* CXIX (December 10, 1924), 637-38.

5. See Crane to Wm. Crane, Nov. 29, 1896, Barrett Collection; Cf. New York *Journal, World, Times,* September 17, 1896; *Press,* Jan. 5, 1897; and scraps of another Crane account of the affair, Clifton Waller Barrett Collection, University of Virginia.

6. See Stephen Crane Scrapbook, Barrett Collection.

7. Lillian Gilkes, *Cora Crane: A Biography of Mrs. Stephen Crane,* 1960 [hereafter "Gilkes"], p. 26.

8. *Ibid.*

9. *Letters,* p. 138.

10. Cf. Day, No. 22.

11. Cf. E. R. Hagemann, " 'Correspondents Three' in the Greco-Turkish War . . ." *American Literature,* XXX (November 1958), 339.

12. "Stephen Crane at Velestino," New York *Journal,* May 11, 1897.

13. "That Was the Romance, The Red Badge of Courage—a Story. This Is the Reality, A Battle Today in Greece—A Fact," New York *Journal,* undated clipping, Syracuse University Library, Stephen Crane Collection.

14. *Work,* XII, 246, 266.

15. John Bass, "How Novelist Crane Acts on the Battlefield," New York *Journal,* May 23, 1897.

16. Quoted in Linson, p. 103.

17. See Thomas F. O'Donnell and Hoyt C. Franchere, *Harold Frederic* (New York, 1961), pp. 65-68.

18. Gilkes, pp. 109-10.

19. Thomas Beer, *Stephen Crane* (1923) [hereafter "Beer"] pp. 160-61.

20. This guess rests on the letter of E. L. Trudeau to Cora Crane, *Letters*, p. 184.

21. *Work*, Vol. XII, p. xiii.

22. "Sayings of the Turret Jacks . . ." *World*, May 15, 1898.

23. "The Red Badge of Courage Was His Wig-Wag Flag," *World*, July 1, 1898.

24. *Notes of a War Correspondent*, 1911, p. 125.

Chapter Three

1. *Bookman*, I (May 1895), 229.

2. Harvey Wickham, "Stephen Crane at College," *American Mercury*, VII (March 1926), 293-94.

3. Stephen Crane pocket notebook, Barrett Collection.

4. *Letters*, p. 110. Cf. n. 31, p. 109, for provenience.

5. In general, see E. H. Cady, *The Gentleman in America* (1949), on the history of this phenomenon.

6. See Cady, No. 11, pp. 30-52.

7. See esp. Roth, No. 49; and Westbrook, No. 63.

8. Beer, p. 140.

9. Cady, No. 11, p. 63.

10. *Scenes and Portraits: Memories of Childhood and Youth* (1954), pp. 124-25.

11. Cf. Helen R. Crane, "My Uncle, Stephen Crane," *American Mercury*, XXXI (January 1934) 26; and Robert H. Davis in *Work*, Vol. II, p. xvii-xix.

12. *Work*, XII, 172.

13. *Work*, XI, 158-59.

14. "Signalling Under Fire," *Work*, IX, 119-20, 123, 125.

15. Letter in the Howells Papers, Houghton Library, Harvard. Published by permission of the Trustees, Remington Art Memorial, Ogdensburg, New York, and of The Houghton Library, Harvard University.

16. Cf. *Letters*, pp. 31, 62, 93, 127.

17. Cf. Remington's enthusiasm for "a romantic literature in America and an art . . . the most romantic of all," in *Letters of Francis Parkman*, ed. by Wibur R. Jacobs, 1960, II, 225.

18. "With Greek and Turk: I. An Impression of the 'Concert,'" *Westminster Gazette*, June [9?], 1897.

19. "My Interview With Soldiers Six," New York *Journal*, June 20, 1897.

20. "The Blue Badge of Cowardice," New York *Journal*, May 12, 1897.

21. "Stephen Crane and Julian Ralph Tell of War's Horrors . . . ," New York *Journal*, May 23, 1897.

22. "How They Leave Cuba: Stephen Crane Describes a Sad Sight," New York *Journal*, October 6, 1898.

23. By T. A. Gullason, "New Light on the Crane-Howells Relationship," *New England Quarterly*, XXX (1957), 389-92.

24. "Stephen Crane Says: Edwin Markham Is His First Choice for the American Academy," New York *Journal*, March 31, 1900.

25. Beer, p. 205.

26. "Hunger Has Made Cubans Fatalists," New York *World*, July 12, 1898.

27. New York *Sun*, May 17, 1896.

28. Beer, p. 140.

29. "With Greek and Turk: VII, The Man in the White Hat," *Westminster Gazette*, June 16, 1897.

30. "Stephen Crane Fears No Blanco," New York *Journal*, August 31, 1898; "Stephen Crane in Havana: He Sees the Comic Side of Things," New York *Journal*, October 9, 1898.

31. "Stephen Crane Says: Watson's Criticisms of England's War Are Not Unpatriotic," New York *Journal*, January 25, 1900.

32. "Regulars Get No Glory," New York *World*, July 20, 1898.

33. "Coney Island's Failing Days," New York *Press* October 14, 1894.

34. "How They Court in Cuba," New York *Journal*, October 25, 1898.

35. Cady, No. 11, pp. 30-32.

36. Linson, p. 37.

37. "Mr. Binks' Day Off: A Study of a Clerk's Holiday," New York *Press*, July 8, 1894.

38. *War Is Kind*, No. XXV.

39. "Ancient Capital of Montezuma," Philadelphia *Press*, July 21, 1895.

40. *Work*, II, 205-6.

41. Cady, No. 11, p. 33.

42. Beer, p. 140.

43. New York *Press*, April 19, 1894.

44. "Coney Island's Failing Days," *loc. cit.*

Chapter Four

1. See Colvert, No. 14.
2. Schoberlin, No. 51, p. 19.
3. Beer, p. 140.
4. See Donald Pizer, "Crane Reports Garland on Howells," *Modern Language Notes*, LXX (January 1955), 37-39.
5. Cf. *The Realist at War . . .* , pp. 212-18.
6. "Realists Must Wait," *New York Times*, October 28, 1894.
7. Stallman, No. 55, p. 14.
8. *Letters*, p. 62.
9. For other views see Stallman, No. 54, and W. B. Stein, No. 58.
10. *Work*, X, 207.
11. *Work*, X, 218.
12. "Life and Letters," *Harper's Weekly*, June 8, 1895.
13. It is doubtful that this and related views will ever be more ably, definitively, even exhaustively, urged and demonstrated than by Ahnebrink, No. 10.
14. Cunliffe, No. 21; and T. A. Gullason, "The Sources of Stephen Crane's *Maggie*," *Philological Quarterly*, XXXVIII (October 1959), 497-502.
15. *Dictionary of American Biography*, II, 504.
16. From Hamlin Garland's first copy of *Maggie* in the Lilly Library, Indiana University. It is printed, with two or three tiny errors of transcription, in *Letters*, p. 14.
17. *Literary History of the United States*, II, 1021.
18. *Letters*, p. 40.
19. James M. Cox, No. 18.
20. *War Is Kind* (1899), p. 41.

Chapter Five

1. *Last Essays* (1926), p. 122. Cf. J. B. Colvert, *"The Red Badge of Courage* and a Review of Zola's *La Débâcle," Modern Language Notes*, LXXI (February 1956), 98-100.
2. See H. T. Webster, "Wilbur F. Hinman's *Corporal Si Klegg* and . . .*The Red Badge of Courage*," *American Literature*, XI (November 1939), 285-93; E. Solomon, "Another Analogue for *The Red Badge of Courage*," *Nineteenth Century Fiction*, XIII (June 1958), 63-66; M. Klotz, "Crane's *The Red Badge of Courage*," *Notes & Queries*, VI (February 1959), 68-69. Cf. E. Stone, "Crane's 'Soldier of the Legion,'" *American Literature*, XXX (May 1958), 242-44.
3. See A. Feldman, "Crane's Title from Shakespeare," *American*

Notes & Queries, VIII (March 1950), 185-86; C. D. Eby, Jr., "The Source of Crane's Metaphor, 'Red Badge of Courage,'" *American Literature,* XXXII (May, 1960).

4. Wickham, p. 295.
5. *Work,* X, 200.
6. Wickham, p. 293.
7. See esp. T. F. O'Donnell, Nos. 43, 44.
8. *Work,* Vol. I, pp. xi-xii.
9. See *New York Tribune,* January 20, 1897, and *Rochester Post Express,* February 22, 1897 (Stephen Crane Scrapbook, Barrett Collection) commenting on H. D. Traill, "The New Realism," *Fortnightly Review,* January 1, 1897.
10. "Editor's Easy Chair," *Harper's Monthly,* CVII (June, 1903), 146-50.
11. "Life and Letters," *Harper's Weekly,* XXXIX (October 26, 1895), 1013.
12. Bass, *op. cit.;* "With Greek and Turk, III," *Westminster Review.*
13. Stallman, No. 55, p. 225 *et seq.*
14. *Work,* I, 50-52.
15. *Ibid.,* p. 70.
16. *Ibid.,* pp. 81-84.
17. Barrett MS, p. 65 ("LV"). Cf. Stallman, No. 55, p. 276.
18. *Work,* I, 86.
19. Barrett Ms, "SV" p. 75 on verso of "LV" p. 118; "SV" p. 76 on verso of "LV" p. 97; "LV" p. 85. (Cf. Stallman, No. 55, pp. 291-92).
20. *Work,* I, 105ff.
21. Barrett MS, "SV" p. 84 on verso of "LV" p. 113; p. 85 on p. 108; p. 86 on p. 112. (Cf. Stallman, No. 55, pp. 298-300).
22. Barrett MS, "LV" p. 125. (Cf. Stallman, No. 55, p. 317).
23. Winifred Lynskey, "Crane's *The Red Badge of Courage,*" *Explicator,* VIII (December 1949), 18. For variant ways of putting the naturalistic argument see also Harry Hartwick, No. 33; and Walcutt, No. 61. J. B. Colvert, No. 15, casts a fresh light on the problem.
24. Stephen Crane Scrapbooks, Barrett Collection.
25. *The New Century Handbook of English Literature* (1956), p. 605; Thrall, Hibbard, and Holman, *A Handbook to Literature* (1960), pp. 237-38.
26. *Willa Cather on Writing* (1949), pp. 35-43.
27. "War Memories," [December 1899] *Work,* IX, 245-46.
28. J. J. Kwiat, No. 37.
29. Linson, pp. 46-47.

30. *Work*, IX, 201.
31. *Work*, I, 59.
32. Gibson, No. 29, p. 5.
33. Charles Feidelson, *Symbolism and American Literature* (1953), esp. pp. 44-76.
34. Hoffman, No. 35, p. xv.
35. *Ibid.*, p. xix.
36. See Osborn, No. 46; Hart, No. 32; Isaac Rosenfeld, "Stephen Crane as Symbolist," *Kenyon Review*, XV (September 1953), 311-14; R. W. Stallman, "The Scholar's Net: Literary Sources," *College English*, XVII (October 1955), 20-27; Stone, No. 60; Carlson, No. 12; Weisberger, No. 62; Greenfield, No. 30; Cox, No. 19; Chase, No. 13.
37. *Work*, Vol. I, p. x.
38. *Work*, I, 98.
39. *Ibid.*, p. 93.
40. *Ibid.*, p. 131.
41. *Ibid.*, pp. 186-87.
42. Stallman, No. 55, pp. 219-21.
43. Solomon, No. 52.
44. *Work*, IX, 238.

Chapter Six

1. *Work*, Vol. IV, p. xii.
2. See Berryman, p. 299ff.
3. *Work*, Vol. IV, p. xi.
4. *Ibid.*, pp. 93-94, 97, 119, 124.
5. Cf. Gilkes, pp. 268-75; Baum, No. 3, pp. 43-44; and *Letters*, p. 344.
6. See esp. Adams, No. 9; Stallman, No. 55, pp. 416-20; Caroline Gordon, "Stephen Crane," *Accent*, IX (September 1949), 153-57; P. Buitenhuis, "The Essentials of Life: 'The Open Boat' as Existentialist Fiction," *Modern Fiction Studies*, V (Autumn, 1959), 243-50; Colvert, No. 15.
7. See esp. Walter Sutton, "Pity and Fear in 'The Blue Hotel,'" *American Quarterly*, IV (Fall, 1952), 73-78; Roth, No. 49; Cox, No. 20; Satterwhite, No. 50; Greenfield, No. 30; Hugh MacClean, "The Two Worlds of 'The Blue Hotel,'" *Modern Fiction Studies*, V (Autumn, 1959), 260-70; Robert F. Gleckner, "Stephen Crane and the Wonder of Man's Conceit," *ibid.*, pp. 271-81; W. B. Stein, "Stephen Crane's *Homo Absurdus*," *Bucknell Review*, VIII (May 1959), 173-74.
8. See Bernard Berenson, *One Year's Reading for Fun*, New York, 1961, pp. 19-23.
9. Liebling, No. 39, p. 72.

Selected Bibliography

A BRIEF ESSAY ON BASIC BOOKS

At the present writing there are at least six basic books indispensable to the study of Stephen Crane. In order of publication, they are:

THOMAS BEER, *Stephen Crane, A Study in American Letters,* New York: Alfred A. Knopf, Inc., 1923. (With introduction by Joseph Conrad).

JOHN BERRYMAN, *Stephen Crane* (American Men of Letters Series), New York: William Sloane Associates, 1950.

DANIEL G. HOFFMAN, *The Poetry of Stephen Crane,* New York: Columbia University Press, 1957.

CORWIN K. LINSON, *My Stephen Crane,* ed. by Edwin H. Cady, Syracuse, New York: Syracuse University Press, 1958.

ROBERT W. STALLMAN and LILLIAN GILKES, *Stephen Crane: Letters,* New York: New York University Press, 1960. (With introduction by Stallman).

LILLIAN GILKES, *Cora Crane: A Biography of Mrs. Stephen Crane,* Bloomington, Indiana: Indiana University Press, 1960.

In Beer, Stephen Crane was both unfortunate and very lucky to find his first biographer. Beer was an elegant cultural historian whose *The Mauve Decade* (1926) and *Hanna* (1929), also concerned with Crane's era, have retained vitality. In spite of corrections and cavils, Beer's remains the central as well as first study of Crane. He had unique access to Crane's contemporaries and exploited them ably. Certain important Crane letters which Beer quoted have not come to light since; and the anecdotes he picked up, now beyond checking, have become the "facts" from which commentators theorize. Later writers chastise Beer for errors they can correct. Yet they accept every unverifiable tale which suits their views—none of us has much recourse. On the whole, Beer's image of Crane has endured. It has been variously embroidered, refined, and refocused. But most efforts to alter it fundamentally expose themselves to charges of intellectual caprice.

On the other hand, Beer's deficiencies are lamentable. Anxious to succeed brilliantly with the biographer's responsibility to art, he ignored his equal obligations to knowledge. As Vincent Starrett pointed out thirty years ago, Beer's "masterpiece" leaves much to be desired: "His impressionism keeps coming between one and what one wants most to know. The book is in actuality a study of the times, in strong light; and across that light moves a somewhat inconspicuous shadow called Stephen Crane."[1] Worse yet, the chiaroscuro leaves many facts (like dates and the succession of events) in the dark, and others in a kind of maddening twilight where one cannot tell whether Beer knows what he is talking about, suspects it to be true, or has invented it.

Into that situation, prevailing despite an accretion of clarifications in the journals during a twenty-year span, stepped the poet John Berryman. As biography, his book was an achievement of courage, tenacity, and detection as well as literary skill. He was faced with an extreme condition of the problem which has bedeviled and distorted Crane studies from the start: the traditions are excruciatingly obscure and contradictory; people sequester important materials and sit on them. It has been frequently remarked that, far beyond those of other writers, problems of research into Crane have been marked by bad temper. Since Berryman's time the following key materials have come into open use by students: the Crouse letters and other holdings now in the Syracuse University Crane Collection, including the Linson manuscript; the magnificent Barrett Collection at the University of Virginia; the Columbia Crane Collection, much of it from Cora Crane's papers; the miscellaneous other items ferreted out by Stallman, Gilkes, Schoberlin, and others. Since then, in short, has occurred the great wave of Crane study and criticism, and Berryman has played a major role in it.

His book is not the definitive Crane biography. Unquestionably we shall have many more Crane studies—whether we ever have the definitive biography may depend on whether, as has been suspected, important new materials are yet to come to light. But it stands beside Beer as an indispensable adjunct. That is true, as I see it, of Berryman as biographer, of most of the first 260 pages of his book. It is not true of him as psychographer and "Freudian" critic, of the scattered theories concerning the provenience and significance of Crane's writing or of the final chapters entitled "Crane's Art" and "The Color of This Soul."[2]

[1] Vincent Starrett, "Stephen Crane: Notes Biographical and Bibliograhical," *Colophon*, II (September 1931), Part 7.

[2] See anon., "Badge of Courage," *Times Literary Supplement* (June 8, 1951), p. 356; D. Aaron, "Stephen Crane," *Hudson Review*, IV (Autumn, 1951), 471-73; M. Blum, "Berryman as Biographer, Stephen Crane as Poet," *Poetry*, LXXVIII (August 1951), 298-307.

As biography, Berryman's Freudian views, especially "The Color of
This Soul," bid fair to establish a popular myth of Crane as foolish
in its way as the nineteenth-century views of Poe and Byron are
in theirs—and for similarly sensational reasons. As the games of lay
psychiatry and the psychoanalysis of long-dead men have become
discredited in intellectual circles, they have become popular in movies,
mass circulation magazines, even TV Westerns. In certain literature
this popularity has been helped by an affinity for fruity sexual description. And in Crane's case this has been brought to a peak by
Mr. Louis Zara. In *Dark Rider* he exercises the privileges of a fictional biographer by appropriating and intensifying a number of
Berryman's ideas and then projecting his own sexual fantasies upon
Crane until the poor author's life reads like a Kinsey case-study.

Given the temper of our times, this is bound to be popular. And
at a popular level there is probably not much use in protesting. But
at a serious level, it certainly ought to be objected that there is, whatever its cause or motive, a great deal of fantasy in this. Serious
"Freudian" biography is fortunately disappearing from the scene.
One doubts that Berryman would have been tempted into it except
for a twin desire to find the "key" to Crane's mystery and to find
something original to add to Beer.

Avoiding the internecine wars of the professionals, there seem to
be two ways to take Freud seriously. The one is the way I think most
people take him now—and will in the future—as a perceptive and sug-
gestive mind which produced a number of enlightening insights into
certain conditions of neurosis and thus significantly affected our
theories of human nature. The other sees Freud as a prophet, the
revealer to mankind of a permanent system of rigid anthropological
truths, all-sufficient for understanding and capable of exegesis but not
alteration—the Gospel according to St. Sigmund, Freudian fundamentalism. Carefully handled, I think the first way of taking Freud,
his successors, disciples, developers, and opponents, may produce
useful insights for the biographer or critic. Fundamentalism, however,
is destructive to both; and some of Berryman's results illustrate
that fact.

To take just one major point, Berryman's case for identifying Crane
with the victims portrayed in Freud's observations on "A Special
Type of Choice of Object made by Men" is very shaky. He plays fast
and loose with the evidence. The sole example, finally, is Cora.
It was not true that Helen Trent and Lily Brandon Munroe were
"sexually discredited" any more than that Crane was in love with
Dora Clark, Doris Watts, or Amy Leslie, or any more than that Crane
fell in love with Cora because he knew of Captain Stewart as a

STEPHEN CRANE

necessary "injured third party." There is no evidence of "an exceptional concern with prostitutes." What has happened is a juggling of evidence to make Crane prove out Freud—the method of the exegete, of the fundamentalist.

This is, it seems to me, an abdication of the responsibility of the biographer. Instead of bringing ideas, information, and insights to elucidate the life, this method employs notions about the life to justify the Master. This same arbitrary, essentially irrelevant method vitiates the criticism, turning it always away from art and back to conjectural biography. It explicates not the literature but the critic's notion of Freudian ideas. Locating the "case" in the literature by fiat, it interprets the case to fit the work and the work to fit the case until it proves triumphantly—the case. Applied by a psychiatrist to a person, that would be a highly suspect method. Applied to a work of literature it is not only suspect, but circular, and, what is worse, non-literary.

One singles out Mr. Berryman in this way partly out of disappointment—a book so good as his would have been a lot better had this all been mitigated—but most of all because he has made himself the fountainhead of this sort of thing in Crane studies. The problems to which he addressed himself—Crane's sexuality, for instance—are difficult and of the utmost importance. It will not do to pretend to solve them by shortcuts, however flamboyant.

Something of the point to that remark is illustrated by Daniel G. Hoffman's excellent *The Poetry of Stephen Crane*. For insight, sensitivity, maturity, breadth of information, originality, and usefulness it must stand in the top rank of doctoral dissertations. Its handling of Crane as poet, his ideas, his sensibility, his "style, sources, symbols," and his relations with poetic tradition have given him a book which will have to be reckoned with for a long time by students of Crane. It rendered obsolete everything previous and is now the starting place for all consideration of the subject. But in his handling of Crane's love-poetry Hoffman adopted Berryman's theories without apparent hesitation. The effect is to leave that part of the question of Crane still wide open for the student of the future.

In this company, the position of Corwin K. Linson's, *My Stephen Crane* is that of a *revenant*. It should have been published before Beer, when it might have excited other surviving intimates to reply or add their testimony to Linson's. Apparently he tried several times in the intervals of a busy painter's life to prepare his memoir for publication, failed repeatedly, and let it lie for many years almost forgotten until the zeal of Lester G. Wells brought it out and it was eventually sold to Syracuse University. Examination of the manuscript showed that, while Linson could write charmingly, he lacked a sense of how to structure a book. Even after the most thorough editing one could give his manuscript without falsifying its character, it had to be published without hope of profit.

A word should perhaps be said about its use. It is uniquely valuable as the eye-witness testimony of an acute and sympathetic man who knew Crane intimately during Crane's obscurest yet artistically most decisive years. It has the deficiencies of error and of limitations of point of view normal to personal accounts. Even more, there is evidence that as Linson aged his own theories of life, and so no doubt of Crane, were altered and his memory accordingly. He has the value, therefore, of the personal but not the disciplined, of the retrospective not the immediate, witness. Nevertheless, there is no other testimony like his.

Robert W. Stallman has been the most active energy in the Crane "field." He has been effective as critic, researcher, bibliographer, editor, and propagandist for a decade; and the end is obviously not yet. One may sometimes disagree with him; there is no denying that he is a force. His finest achievement to date, however, is his part in gathering the *Letters*. They are relatively few in number even for a career so short as Crane's, and there is always the possibility— the hope—that substantially more may appear. Meanwhile, for all one could wish the number of letters was greater and the provenience of some texts more securely established by originals, he and Miss Gilkes have provided us with the single most advanced and reliable tool for Crane research yet produced. The careful student will wish to take note of the footnotes and "Catalogue" materials on the sources of the texts. Hopefully, this volume of *Letters* may be superseded some day by a better one. But it will be a hard-digging and a lucky scholar who does the job. And in what is apt to be a long meanwhile, we may be very grateful for what we have been given.

That the vexing problem of Crane's sexuality is not solved by the current guesswork is evidenced by the reluctance to treat it on the part of his "wife's" biographer. No doubt for lack of facts, Lillian Gilkes's marvelously researched *Cora Crane*, from which much might have been hoped in this direction, brings us no nearer solution. This is the more striking in that, even with the windfall of Cora's papers at Columbia, Miss Gilkes's success in uncovering the where-withal to revive a life so little understood and apparently lost is phenomenal. Alfred Kazin, for instance, praises her book as one "that really helps us to see people of another epoch—how they lived and what they thought about."[3] Along the way, she has provided a number of fresh facts and sidelights on the life of Stephen Crane. It was a difficult book to write and a correspondingly admirable achievement. To judge largely from the author's own appended accounts of her struggles with sources, however, not all the difficulties may have been so triumphantly mastered as at first glance appears. She seems to have made some arbitrary decisions about the dates, handwriting, authorship, and perhaps the meaning of some very ambiguous documents. Nor is her treatment of Cora's "husband" impeccable.

Miss Gilkes's attitude toward Stephen, in fact, comes through as characteristically what lawyers call "adversary." She defends Cora by denigrating Crane. Like most good biographers, she has fallen in love with her subject. She seems to wish to ignore the fact emphasized in her title, as in the structure of the book. Had the title been something like "Cora Howorth Murphy Stewart (alias Taylor), Bluestocking Madam," practically nobody would care. Nevertheless, from Miss Gilkes's point of view, Cora can do no real wrong. Did she make money off the flesh, nerves, and psyches of her girls? Well, at least in 1896 they didn't sleep in. Did Crane make efforts to escape from her? He was a heel. The possibilities that Cora may have been fatal to Crane's art and health are never entertained: Cora was literary too.

PRIMARY SOURCES

Because of limited space, the works of Crane listed in the Chronology are not repeated in this section.

The standard and sole "collected" text is *The Work of Stephen Crane*, edited by Wilson Follett, 1925-1926, and published in 750 sets by Alfred A. Knopf. Each volume is well introduced; especially important are the essays by Hergesheimer, Vol. I; R. H. Davis, Vol. II; Carl Van Doren, Vol. IV; Amy Lowell, Vol. VI; Willa Cather, Vol. IX; Charles Michelson, Vol. XII. For more recent editions see esp. Nos. 13, 29, 35, 38, 51, and 55, below.

SECONDARY SOURCES

I. *Bibliographical*

1. WILLIAMS, AMES, and VINCENT STARRETT. *Stephen Crane, a Bibliography*, Glendale, Calif.: John Valentine, 1948. Needs thorough updating and redoing.

[3] "Stephen Crane's Scarlet Woman," *Reporter*, XXIII (November 24, 1960), 53-54, 56.

2. BLANCK, JACOB. *Bibliography of American Literature*, II, New Haven: Yale University Press, 1957, 329-38. Identification of all S.C.'s separate (non-periodical) publications, plus non-periodical publications about him, to 1956.

3. BAUM, JOAN H. *Stephen Crane: An Exhibition of His Writings* . . . , New York: Columbia University Libraries, 1956. Many interesting additions to Crane bibliography.

4. STALLMAN, ROBERT W. "Stephen Crane: Some New Stories," *Bulletin of the New York Public Library*, LX and LXI (September 1956, October 1956, January 1957), 455-62, 477-486, 36-46. Previously unpublished materials from the Barrett Collection.

5. STALLMAN, ROBERT W. " 'The Red Badge of Courage': A Collation of Two Pages of Manuscript Expunged from Chapter XII," *Papers of the Bibliographical Society of America*, IXL (No. 3, 1955), 273-77.

6. RANDALL, D. A., and J. T. WINTERICH. "One Hundred Good Novels—Crane, Stephen: *The Red Badge of Courage*," *Publishers' Weekly*, CXXXVI (October 21, 1939), 1625-26.

7. BEEBE, MAURICE, and THOMAS A. GULLASON. "Criticism of Stephen Crane: A Selected Checklist with an Index to Studies of Separate Works," *Modern Fiction Studies*, V (Autumn, 1959), 282-91.

8. See also Berryman and Hoffman above; Lettis, Stallman and Gilkes below.

II *Critical*

9. ADAMS, RICHARD P. "Naturalistic Fiction: 'The Open Boat,' " *Tulane Studies in English*, IV (1954), 137-46.

10. ÅHNEBRINK, LARS. *The Beginnings of Naturalism in American Fiction: A Study of the Works of Hamlin Garland, Stephen Crane, and Frank Norris with Special Reference to Some European Influences, 1891-1903*, Upsala, Sweden, Lundequitska, 1950. An admirably thorough, scholarly, energetic, wide-ranging doctoral dissertation, full of original observation and fascinating citations. Relies perhaps too heavily on the evidential technique of the "deadly parallel."

11. CADY, EDWIN H., and LESTER G. WELLS, eds. *Stephen Crane's Love Letters to Nellie Crouse*, Syracuse, New York: Syracuse University Press, 1954. Photographs and documents, the commentary and bibliographies, make this still useful.

12. CARLSON, ERIC W. "Crane's *The Red Badge of Courage*, IX,"

Explicator, XVI (March 1958), number 34. The "red wafer" as a non-Christian seal.

13. CHASE, RICHARD. *"The Red Badge of Courage" and Other Writings by Stephen Crane,* Boston: Houghton Mifflin, 1960. One of the best general editions. Excellent introduction.

14. COLVERT, JAMES B. "The Origins of Stephen Crane's Literary Creed," *University of Texas Studies in English,* XXXIV (1955), 179-88. Crane's transit from Kipling and "The Light That Failed" toward the creed of Howells and Garland.

15. COLVERT, JAMES B. "Style and Meaning in Stephen Crane: 'The Open Boat,'" *University of Texas Studies in English,* XXXVII (1958), 34-45.

16. CONRAD, JOSEPH. "His War Book," Preface to *The Red Badge of Courage* (1925), pp. v-xii. *The Red Badge* as a masterpiece.

17. CONRAD, JOSEPH. "Stephen Crane: A Note Without Dates," *London Mercury,* I (December 1919), 192-93. Personal impressions twenty years after.

18. COX, JAMES M. *"The Pilgrim's Progress* as a Source for Stephen Crane's *The Black Riders,"* *American Literature,* XXVIII (January, 1957), 478-87.

19. COX, JAMES T. "The Imagery of *The Red Badge of Courage,"* *Modern Fiction Studies,* V (Autumn, 1959), 209-19. A key essay in the debate over Crane's symbolism.

20. COX, JAMES T. "Stephen Crane as Symbolic Naturalist: An Analysis of 'The Blue Hotel,'" *Modern Fiction Studies,* III (Summer, 1957), 147-58.

21. CUNLIFFE, MARCUS. "Stephen Crane and the American Background of *Maggie,"* *American Quarterly,* VII (Spring 1955), 31-44.

22. DAY, CYRUS. "Stephen Crane and the Ten-foot Dinghy," *Boston University Studies in English,* III (1957), pp. 193-213. Argues persuasively that it was a nicer day and a shorter row ashore when the *Commodore* sank than has been supposed. Argues less persuasively that somehow those facts invalidate the achievement of "The Open Boat": good seamanship, weak criticism.

23. DICKASON, DAVID H. "Stephen Crane and the *Philistine,"* *American Literature,* XV (November 1943), 279-87. A sound summary of the relationship with Elbert Hubbard.

24. FEIDELSON, CHARLES, JR. "Three Views of the Human Person: *The Scarlet Letter, Walden,* and *The Red Badge of Courage,"* *Reports and Speeches of The Sixth Yale Conference on The Teaching of English,* April 8 and 9, 1960, pp. 47-52. On Henry

Fleming's assumption of the burdens of becoming and being human.

25. FORD, FORD MADOX. "Stevie and Co.," *New York Essays* (New York, W. E. Rudge 1927), pp. 21-32. Reminiscence, especially of Crane and Henry James. Ford's theories of Crane.

26. FRANCHERE, RUTH. *Stephen Crane: The Story of an American Writer*, New York, Crowell, 1961. Excellently written, fictionalized "juvenile" biography. Strong on Crane's pain, his irresponsibility; well researched.

27. FRIEDMAN, NORMAN. "Criticism and the Novel: Hardy, Hemingway, Crane, Woolf, Conrad," *Antioch Review*, XVIII (1958), 343-70. An important effort to make sense of the novel and the modes of criticism of the 1950's by, in part, reflecting *The Red Badge* and its criticism upon each other.

28. GEISMAR, MAXWELL. *Rebels and Ancestors: The American Novel, 1890-1915*, Boston, Houghton Mifflin, 1953, 69-136. Mainly notable for placing Crane in the author's picture of the development of the modern American novel and for explications more orthodoxly Freudian than Berryman's.

29. GIBSON, WILLIAM M., ed. *Stephen Crane: Selected Prose and Poetry*, 1950; rev. ed., *Stephen Crane: "The Red Badge of Courage" and Selected Prose and Poetry*, New York, Rinehart, 1956. One of the best editions, excellent introduction.

30. GREENFIELD, STANLEY B. "The Unmistakable Stephen Crane," *PMLA*, LXXIII (December, 1958), 562-72. Opposition to what the author regards as irresponsible symbolistic readings of Crane.

31. HAGEMANN, EDWARD R. "Crane's 'Real' War in His Short Stories," *American Quarterly*, VIII (1956), 356-67. A serious, important effort to analyze Crane's vision of war.

32. HART, JOHN E. "*The Red Badge of Courage* as Myth and Symbol," *University of Kansas City Review*, XIX (Summer, 1953), 249-56. An attempted reading in Jungian terms.

33. HARTWICK, HARRY. "The Red Badge of Nature," *The Foreground of American Fiction*, New York, American Book Co., (1934), pp. 21-44. A caricature of Crane as "naturalist."

34. HEMINGWAY, ERNEST. *The Green Hills of Africa*, 1935. A tribute and possibly an acknowledgement of indebtedness. Cf. P. Young, *Ernest Hemingway*, 1952, pp. 161-69.

35. HOFFMAN, DANIEL G., ed. *"The Red Badge of Courage" and Other Stories by Stephen Crane*, New York, Harper, 1957. Though regrettably limited to war stories, a good edition with a valuable introduction.

36. KINDILIEN, CARLIN T. "Stephen Crane and the 'Savage Philosophy' of Olive Schreiner," *Boston University Studies in English*, III (1957), 97-107. Conjectural influence study.

37. KWIAT, JOSEPH J. "Stephen Crane and Painting," *American Quarterly*, IV (Winter 1952), 331-38. The definitive argument for an influence from Impressionism in painting upon Crane.

38. LETTIS, RICHARD, R. F. McDONNEL, and W. E. MORRIS. *Stephen Crane's "The Red Badge of Courage," Text and Criticism*, New York, Harcourt Brace, 1960. A "controlled research" sort of volume, reprinting the novel and some hundred pages of critical excerpts, including materials from various items on this list.

39. LIEBLING, A. J. "The Dollars Damned Him," *The New Yorker*, August 5, 1961, 48-72. Theorizes that it was a "Western Conformist Protestant" bourgeois anxiety about money, nothing else, which killed Crane. Memorable side-comments on other critics.

40. MILNE, W. GORDON. "Stephen Crane: Pioneer in Technique," *Die Neueren Sprachen*, VIII (July 1959), 297-303. On Crane's style, especially his "explosive kind of imagery."

41. MARCUS, MORDECAI. "The Unity of *The Red Badge of Courage*," original essay for Lettis, No. 38, pp. 189-95. A valuable effort to sum up.

42. MARCUS, MORDECAI and ERIC MARCUS. "Animal Imagery in *The Red Badge of Courage*," *Modern Language Notes*, LXXIV (February 1959), 108-11.

43. O'DONNELL, THOMAS F. "De Forest, Van Petten, and Stephen Crane," *American Literature*, XXVII (January, 1956), 578-80.

44. O'DONNELL, THOMAS F. "John B. Van Petten: Stephen Crane's History Teacher," *American Literature*, XXVII (May 1955), 196-202.

45. OSBORN, SCOTT C. "The 'Rivalry-Chivalry' of Richard Harding Davis and Stephen Crane," *American Literature*, XXVIII (March 1956), 50-61. Especially on the question of whether Davis modeled his "A Derelict" in *Ranson's Folly*, 1927, on Crane.

46. OSBORN, SCOTT C. "Stephen Crane's Imagery: 'Pasted Like a Wafer,'" *American Literature*, XXIII (November 1951), 362. Possible debt to Kipling.

47. PIZER, DONALD. "The Garland-Crane Relationship," *Huntington Library Quarterly*, XXIV (November 1960), 75-82. A keen and very useful disentangling of a badly snarled skein of relationships.

48. ROSS, LILLIAN. "Onward and Upward With the Arts," *New*

Yorker, XXVIII (May 24, May 31, June 7, June 14, and June 21, 1952), 32-87, 29-71, 32-79, 39-65, 31-83. The making of the movie from *The Red Badge.*

49. ROTH, RUSSEL. "A Tree in Winter: The Short Fiction of Stephen Crane," *New Mexico Quarterly,* XXIII (Summer, 1953), 188-96. Crane as "puritan" and "classicist."

50. SATTERWHITE, JOSEPH N. "Stephen Crane's 'The Blue Hotel': The Failure of Understanding," *Modern Fiction Studies,* II (Winter, 1956-1957), 238-41.

51. SCHOBERLIN, MELVIN, ed. *The Sullivan County Sketches of Stephen Crane,* Syracuse, New York, Syracuse University Press, 1949. A beautifully edited and illustrated (by George Vander Sluis) volume. The introduction is excellent and sustains the hope that Schoberlin's long awaited biography of Crane may yet appear.

52. SOLOMON, ERIC. "A Gloss on *The Red Badge of Courage,*" *Modern Language Notes,* LXXV (February, 1960), 111-13. On "The Veteran."

53. SOLOMON, ERIC. "The Structure of *The Red Badge of Courage,*" *Modern Fiction Studies,* V (Autumn, 1959), 220-34. A complex, well-controlled, and intelligent critique.

54. STALLMAN, ROBERT W. "Crane's *Maggie:* a Reassessment," *Modern Fiction Studies,* V (Autumn, 1959), 251-59. Analysis of form.

55. STALLMAN, ROBERT W., ed. *Stephen Crane, an Omnibus,* New York, Alfred A. Knopf, Inc., 1952. An exciting, pioneering work on its appearance, this has been superseded—in large part by Stallman's subsequent work. Still interesting for *Red Badge* text and critical ideas.

56. STALLMAN, ROBERT W. "Stephen Crane's Primrose Path," *New Republic,* CXXXIII (September 19, 1955), 17-18. On *Maggie.*

57. STALLMAN, ROBERT W. "Stephen Crane's Revision of *Maggie: A Girl of the Streets,*" *American Literature,* XXVI (January 1955), 528-36.

58. STEIN, WILLIAM BYSSHE. "New Testament Inversions in Crane's *Maggie,*" *Modern Language Notes,* LXXIII (April 1958), 268-72. Becomes "inverted" enough to argue that Maggie represents Christ.

59. "Stephen Crane—Special Number," *Modern Fiction Studies,* V (Autumn 1959), 199-291. An extraordinarily successful "special," a good sampler of recent criticism.

60. STONE, EDWARD. "The Many Suns of *The Red Badge of Courage,*" *American Literature,* XXIX (November 1957), 322-26.

61. WALCUTT, CHARLES C. "Stephen Crane: Naturalist and Impressionist," in *American Literary Naturalism, a Divided Stream,* Minneapolis, University of Minnesota Press, (1956), pp. 66-86. What might have been the definitive argument is weakened by the author's inclination to beg his terms and the question of their applicability to the literature.

62. WEISBERGER, BERNARD. *"The Red Badge of Courage," Twelve Original Essays,* edited by Charles Shapiro (Detroit, Wayne State University Press, 1958), 96-123. An ambitious, perhaps too condensed, effort to cover a complex subject in brief. Worth attention.

63. WESTBROOK, MAX. "Stephen Crane: The Pattern of Affirmation," *Nineteenth Century Fiction,* XIV (December 1959), 219-29. A careful, interesting analysis of Crane's ideas.

64. ZARA, LOUIS. *Dark Rider: A Novel Based on the Life of Stephen Crane,* New York, World, 1961. Full of often brilliant guesses, after a Freudian mode different from Berryman's, this makes an exciting, sometimes commercialized, account of the life. Makes Crane's art seem largely irrelevant.

Index

Index

Index